DRIVEN BY LOVE

From Islam to Christ

EMMANUEL NESTER

WestBow Press books may be ordered through booksellers or by contacting:

WestBow Press
A Division of Thomas Nelson & Zondervan
1663 Liberty Drive
Bloomington, IN 47403
www.westbowpress.com
1 (866) 928-1240

ISBN: 978-1-5127-2543-8 (sc)
ISBN: 978-1-5127-2544-5 (hc)
ISBN: 978-1-5127-2542-1 (e)

Library of Congress Control Number: 2016900073

Print information available on the last page.

WestBow Press rev. date: 01/25/2016

CONTENTS

INTRODUCTION

A world view that made perfect sense ordered his daily life. He navigated every uncertain alley with confidence in what he knew to be truth. He was on a fast track to places most young men would never even imagine. Then with the fateful turn of a card everything he knew to be true would be turned upside down. The solid rock upon which he was so safely grounded would be shattered.

However when he came face to face with the truth it finally hit him. And all the many doubts he had suppressed like invisible hair-like cracks in a great dark crystal, suddenly exploded into giant caverns of unapproachable light brilliantly revealing the truth with diamond clarity.

Out of the blackness of hate and lies, his life would forever change. A new birth and a new life in Christ driven by love.

PREFACE

This book is about the journey I have been on ever since I gave my life to Jesus Christ, after fourteen years of being a Muslim. I go back to my childhood to show my readers how different I was from other Muslim kids around me, and later how that difference played a huge part in me giving my life to Christ.

The book is not just about telling my story, but sharing God's story and also the lessons God has taught me on this journey, through the different people and experiences I have been through. So through this book I use my story to share God's story that is why you will see a lot of scriptures.

The way I write this book portrays a lot about who I am and how I think, ever since I became a Christian, God gave me a hunger to stand and preach His word. That preacher in me will come out in different parts of this book. After moving from Africa to Korea, I have had a chance to read about and see many churches through internet or in person. Many churches are practicing what Doctor Michael Horton calls "Christless Christianity," churches preoccupied with being practical, well liked and successful at the expense of the truth of the Gospel. In different portions of the book I talk about these churches.

And finally as we often do in Uganda, I have followed the typical Ugandan way of telling stories, I have mixed all the above, my story, God's story, lessons learned, and my experiences, but all these to point to one thing which is LOVE.

This is my first book, enjoy reading it.

CHAPTER 1

EYES OF A CHILD

Life in Uganda is very communal. Families raise their children together. Women farm together. Men drink together. And in our village, Bugembe, in eastern Uganda, the children walked to and from school in large clusters like bees to flowers in the summertime.

I do not have many memories of my life as a baby, but from what I have heard, I was a cute, chubby little boy. Everyone loved to hold me. My mom never had a problem carrying her chubby baby everywhere because she had the help of everyone else around her. Some babies might be picky over who carries them, but I embraced whoever would feed me. I loved to eat; loved it so much that I cried between spoonfuls. After a full belly, I would hold onto them and sleep soundly in their arms

I grew up hearing stories about how my aunts, sisters, and neighbors loved me as a baby. But I heard very little about my dad loving me. As a matter of fact, whenever I flipped through the photo albums, I remember seeing very few pictures of my dad holding me. I did not understand why that was the case. It could have been because my father had several other wives and other kids to worry about. In a heavily Muslim town like Bugembe, a man could up to four wives, for example my father had four. With all those wives and at least seven children, maybe I was just one among many. Or maybe he was just too busy. In any case, the truth was that at this early stage of my life, there's not much to say about me and my father.

You've heard the adage, "It takes a village to raise a child." This phrase comes from Africa, by the way. When I played with the village children, other parents and elders watched over me, and other times, my family would watch the other children while playing with me. Although we were generally supervised, we were free to roam, to play, to find others, to explore the world together. Outside the kindergarten classroom, we weren't trapped at home with our parents, expected to learn piano or study for an exam. Instead, we were just allowed to be kids—unscheduled, unstructured, and outside. That's how I met my childhood friend, Peace.

Peace was my best friend. I thought Peace was the most beautiful girl in the village. Typically, five-year-old boys would rather spend their time killing birds, by throwing rocks, fighting with each other and bullying everyone else. But I wasn't a typical boy; I preferred spending time with Peace rather than stoning birds. However, I was not the only boy that wanted to spend time with Peace.

At my kindergarten, one boy was taller, older, and stronger than the others, and he was meaner too. His name was Asheraf, and he was a bully. He picked on anyone smaller than he was, like me, but he also picked on the girls, and he picked on my best friend Peace. When I stood up for Peace, he picked on her more, just to show me that he was bigger and stronger. Part of me wanted to stand up to Asheraf one time, to fight him and teach him not to mess with Peace. But this was only a wishful thinking, because I knew that would be the end of me if I dared to fight him. He was a kindergarten Goliath and we all feared him. One time, I had had enough of his bullying, and I stepped in to protect her. It was the first fight of my life, and it was more of a beat-down than a real fight, with Asheraf doing the beating. From that early age, I knew the difference between fighting to hurt and fighting to protect something, and I knew I was different from the other boys.

Peace and I lived a four minute walk away from each other. Every day at school I could not wait for that time the bell rang to send us home, so Peace and I could walk home together. We usually carried food to school to eat during break time but I always carried some extra to share with

Peace. When I met with other boys I spent so much of the time telling them about Peace, and as a little boy I imagined that Peace and I would always be together and have a family like my mom and dad had. I imagined that sometime I would eventually become big enough to be able to fight the bully Asheraf and I would have Peace all to myself. For a small boy, I was thinking big, and when I shared these plans with my friends they just made fun of me.

When the bell rang at the end of the school day, I would linger outside waiting for Peace with the hope of walking her home. Peace's family was one of the wealthiest in town, even wealthier than mine, so sometimes her brother would pick her up in the shiny black car. Those were the days my heart would sink as she drove away, and I would have to walk home with the boys. Every day I watched and waited, hoping that black car wouldn't come so we could spend time together walking home.

One morning at school, we got into class but noticed something strange—Peace was not there. I was sad, but maybe she was sick and I'd see her the next day. The next day Peace was absent again. The whole week went by and Peace didn't return to school. After two weeks without Peace, I learnt she was never going to come back to our small kindergarten. She had moved to a better school in the capital city, more than three hours away. I was hurt. I did not want to go to school anymore. Everything seemed to sour from that point on, and I moped around without Peace. My friends started making fun of me, and Asheraf bullied me even more. I had no one to share my food with, and I just didn't want to go back to school without Peace.

Without Peace, I started to hang with the boys and do what boys do. But I was not the best at whatever they did. We finished class one day and on our way home we decided to play in the trees like we saw the monkeys do. The problem was we were not good enough, or at least I was not good enough, to do what monkeys did. It only took a few swings on a tree limb before it broke off and I came falling down to the ground like rain. After that landing, I decided that monkey swinging wasn't such a good idea, and I decided to leave my friends and walk home. Little did I know, my fall had actually dislocated my elbow. On my way home, my elbow started aching a little and swelling, so I tried to hide it from my mom. But mothers only need one look at their child's face to know something is wrong, and she called me wanting to know why I was hiding my arm. By that time, my elbow and forearm had swollen up like a balloon and I was in a lot of pain, and she knew something was very wrong.

The next morning, the local medicine man paid us a visit. He spread herbs and other local medicine on my arm and massaged it in—a painful treatment. However, when my grandmother heard about what the local medicine man was doing, she fetched me from the village and brought me to the larger town where a better doctor treated my arm. While injuring my arm was a disaster at the time, it allowed me to pull out of that kindergarten and spend time at my grandmother's house healing. Why was that a good thing? With Peace not at school, kindergarten was no longer fun for me, and I had no reason to want to go.

My grandmother took good care of me. She was my father's mother, and aside from my father, grandmother only had daughters. In turn, her daughters had all daughters. I was the only boy in the family, and therefore, the sole male heir. If one of my sisters had fallen from a tree, she might not have received the same amount of care. I was treated with love and tenderness by my grandmother who saw me hurting and took me out of my pain. She reminded me of this incident many times later, when I was misbehaving or causing trouble, that I owed it to her to act better. Almost ten years later, I became a follower of Christ. This brought her much disappointment and shame, and she reminded me of that incident again. "You were in so much pain. You could have been crippled and I saved you. Is this how you repay that kindness—with bringing shame on me and the family?"

CHAPTER 2

THE TOWN SCHOOL

I was laid up for about a month at my grandmother's house, and then it was time to get back in school. I enrolled in a new school in the town as a Primary One student (British education system, Primary one is same Elementary School in the American education system), but my classmates were so different than the kids at my village kindergarten. However, I was happy to have a fresh start with new students who didn't know me or my background with Peace. And they didn't know me well enough to tease me yet. Although I would make more friends, I never had another one quite like Peace my entire time at this new school. Whenever I was back in my village during vacation, I would walk by Peace's house to see if she had come back from the capital. Sadly, I never saw her again.

When I was home in the village, I found myself drawn to working with the animals—my goats, sheep, and chickens. They listened to me and loved me. When they first saw me coming, they would get excited, and when I called them they came to me. My animals would mix with other people's animals to graze, and the animals looked alike and usually didn't have tags or collars. But when time came to go home, I made my sound and all my animals rushed over to me. I spent most of my leisure time in the bush with my goats. People around the village would give me their goats to go graze them, and I would bring back those happy goats in the evening with full stomachs. When I went out to play, I would return home with all sorts of new animals—birds, cats, and puppies, to name a few—but my parents wanted nothing to do with these animals. If they'd let me, I would have started my own zoo.

Meanwhile, I was learning the differences between my new town school and my old village school. For one thing, at the village kindergarten I never wore shoes, and that was just fine for a five-year-old. But I had to wear shoes at the town school. They were very uncomfortable, and I couldn't walk straight, but I had to wear them anyway. My father bought me new shorts to wear to school to comply with the school dress code. I was still small, and the shorts were so big that they swallowed my legs like a pleated skirt, and I felt like the whole school was making fun of me. But there was no way I could tell my father that I did not like the shorts that he had bought for me. In Uganda, a gift was a gift, and it was wrong to criticize it, especially if that gift was from my father. Whenever I wore those shorts to school, the other kids laughed at me as soon as I walked into the classroom. The shorts and the shoes were uncomfortable, and they were also making my social life miserable. I already stood out at school because I was the shortest in my class and had a big nose; it didn't help matters that the town kids could tell just by the way I dressed that I was the village boy. I didn't need any more problems.

It didn't take long before I began to hate going to school. So I just stopped going. Instead I would go play in town by myself during school hours, and then go home at the usual time. At the end of the school term, when students were supposed to present report cards to their parents, of course I had nothing to present. My father visited the school to fetch the report card and there he learnt that I had not been attending school for the last month. That night, I ran to my grandmother's house because I knew it was the safest place to hide from my father. I thought my grandmother loved me too much to surrender me to my father's punishment, but he came anyway right to where he knew I would be-- under the bed at my grandmother's house. He took me back home and gave me a whooping. By a whooping I do not mean a light spanking, I mean a real whooping with a tree branch. This was the first whooping I ever got from my father. Before this, only my mother had whooped me, she was the main administrator of punishment. In Uganda it is a great pride to have a son, so naturally I felt that my father was so proud of me and loved me too much to punish me. But I found out the truth when I stopped going to school.

My decision to skip school, and my father's reaction, became a major turning point in my life. My father decided to send me away to a boarding school so that I wouldn't have the option to skip school again. The school was in a village about two hours away from my home, and for the whole school term I was locked inside the school grounds. There was no going outside to play or herd my goats or see the people I loved most. Life at the boarding school was horrible. It felt like a prison.

The only thing to look forward to at the boarding school was visitation day. Twice a term, my family could come and visit me, and it meant a great deal to me and the other students to finally see our families. It was like Christmas for the boarding school boys—we knew our families would bring gifts and home-cooked food, a real treat from the tasteless school food. I didn't sleep the night before visitation day; I was just too wound up with anticipation. Very early in the morning, I got dressed and sat by the window, waiting and watching the gate to see if my parents were the next people to enter the school ground. I watched students run full of excitement when they saw their parents. The hugging and smiling made me even more anxious to see my own parents walk through the gate. But sometimes they didn't come.

There were several times when I woke up early, was dressed and watching the gate by 9 AM I watched the minutes go by and then hours. Noon came, then 3 PM, still hopeful. By 6 PM, it started getting dark and I gave up hope of seeing my family that day. My hurt was made worse by the contrast to the other kids, who were having the time of their lives with their families. Everyone showed off what their families had brought for them, and I had nothing to show. The other students had all eaten good homemade food, and I was among the few who eventually had to give up waiting for our families and eat the tasteless cafeteria "posho," the starchy mashed maize. My pain was only heightened because my anticipation was so high. From that time on, I started training myself not to expect much from others so that I wouldn't be let down.

My father was rich by Ugandan standards. He owned at least three cars and a couple of houses. I never saw him take the public bus or even sit on a bicycle. Truth be told, he was richer than most parents who came to visit their children at the boarding school. My father only lived two hours away, but my family was often absent on visitation day, while other parents who lived twice as far away never failed to visit. Some students didn't need to guess or worry whether their parents would visit. They simply knew they would come, so the kids played or took naps patiently waiting for the call that their families had arrived. I didn't have that luxury. After many visitation days spent alone, waiting in vain, I knew not to get my hopes up.

It was not all bad. On those occasions when my father came to visit, he came later in the evening. It was good that he did visit, but we never were able to sit down and talk or even eat together. Sometimes my waiting was not for nothing. Sometimes my mom did walk through that gate, and when she did, she always brought gifts. We sat and ate together and later I had something to brag about to my friends. These were some of the best memories I have with my family. Just by visiting me at school, I felt that they loved me so much.

Visitation days were great for seeing families, but at the same time, they were a chance for our parents to see our grades. Out of some ninety students, I was one of the youngest, but I managed to work my way up to the 3rd highest rank in the class. I was looking forward to showing this off to my parents, thinking they would be proud that I had made such progress. But when my father saw that I was only third, and not first, he was disappointed. He would only accept the very best, and I let him down. I saw other parents on visitation day overjoyed with their kids who were ranked in the top half of the class. I never understood my father's disappointment. I wanted his approval, his understanding. I wanted him to focus on what I had done right, not what I had done wrong.

When I came home on vacation from boarding school, my mom was excited for me to look after some rabbits that she had bought while I was away. She knew I loved animals, and now I could take care of them for her. But that boarding school changed me. I did not love animals like I used too. I was different now, and I didn't want to go into the bush with goats anymore. My mom was disappointed with my new attitude, and disappointed that I wouldn't be taking care of her rabbits.

I don't know if that was a natural change or not. I felt like I had been separated from the things I loved most in my childhood: first Peace, then my family, and finally the animals. It seemed like my love for these things just faded away or died. When I came back home from boarding school I started to run with the boys and do boy stuff. I played with fire, I enjoyed killing chickens, and I stoned dogs for fun. Before I went to boarding school, I loved animals, but now I preferred to hurt them. I got into fights on a regular basis. I was a different kid.

I also complained a lot about boarding school and how much I hated it, but my father did not like hearing that. He thought I was soft, and wanted me to be a stronger boy instead of acting like a whiny girl. He became even harsher with me now than before. Over time he started showing me less and less kindness and more and more anger. He was never too busy to drop something important to give me a whooping and teach me a lesson, but when I did well, he was strangely too busy to say, "Well done, son" or "Good job." He stopped referring to me as son, or other nicknames fathers have for their sons. Instead he just called me the impersonal "you," or he used my given name. In our culture, this was usually reserved for times of accusation and punishment. By this time, I was about seven years old. I don't know if I had also transformed into a different person after boarding school, but he certainly was not the same dad that I had known before.

Growing up I never heard my father say, "I love you son." He never hugged me, he never held my hand to cross the road together, and he never made time for those normal things like playing soccer or teaching me something new. But the most painful thing of all is that my father made plenty of time for other village boys. He would take them for a ride in one of the cars for no reason at all. He joked around and played with them, but never with me. It was always very painful when these boys came to tell me, "Dude, your dad is really cool. Your dad just did this and that for me." These boys knew my father better than I did. I never knew why it was easier for my father to spend more time with other village boys than with his own son.

CHAPTER 3

A NOTE TO LOVED ONES

About ten years down the road, I find myself in Seoul, Korea. I have been here the past five years, and it has been interesting to watch parents and their children. As I see and interact with Korean kids, I can't help but look back at when I was a small boy. I make comparisons between them and myself, but our differences outweigh our similarities by a big margin. The kids here have it far better than I did. The kids I see here get to hear, see and feel that love from their parents. I have seen kids that are truly treated like a precious gift, the girls are princesses, and the boys are princes—or all the other lovely names out there. The parents express love better through the hugs, the gifts, bed time stories, going to movies, baseball games, birthday parties, playing in the park and more. Korean mothers just love their kids, it almost makes me jealous. About three years ago, I started helping out a young boy, who was learning English. His mother always came with him, and she bragged a lot about this boy. It puzzled me how this mother could be so proud of a boy whose English was grade F quality. My life was the direct opposite. If I had a choice as a little boy maybe I would have chosen their lives instead of mine. Maybe I would have picked their parents over mine. I know my parents loved me; it was very evident when I was very sick in the hospital. However, the difference was they really never told me they loved me. I had to try and figure that out on my own.

Maybe if the Korean kids were to write about love, they would have a better life story account than mine. It is so amazing sometimes; I feel like

I am watching a movie. However, I am equally amazed at the fact that some of these kids do not know how good they have it. I am amazed at how ungrateful, selfish and rude some of these kids can be. To me having such parental love and care would mean the world. It would be the most precious thing in my life.

It's almost painful to hear a father call his daughter, "Baby come here," and hear her say, "I DON'T WANT TO." I saw a boy with his dad at a toy shop. His dad bought him a toy, but the boy tossed it to the ground because it was not the specific gift he wanted. On the subway I saw another boy yelling and swinging punches at his mother. If I ever did that in Uganda I would be in heaven with grandma. Part of me wishes I could trade life with these kids for just a week. Just a week to hear, see and feel love. Just a week to hold Mom and Dad's hand as we walk through the park. Just a week to hear the bed time stories, to get the hugs, to be called "my love." Just a week and I would forever be grateful.

I have noticed that in developed countries a lot of kids grow up with the spirit of entitlement and lose the spirit of gratitude. Kids grow up thinking, *Of course my parents have to love me, of course my parents have to put me through school, and they have to give me this and that.* So, instead of being thankful for the things they have, they whine and cry about the things they do not have. After the life I have been through, and the things I have seen in Uganda, I know that we are not entitled to love, school, gifts or shelter from our parents.

There are parents who give up on their kids long before they make it out of the womb. These parents choose to kill their kids instead of bringing them into the world. But if you are here it means your parents did not give up on you, especially your mother. She decided to go through all the pain to bring you in this world. Where I come from, a lot of mothers die from childbirth complications. Others get very sick. A mother is put out of her comfort zones to bring that baby into the world, yet she still does it for the sake of the baby. We are not entitled to that. Though my love story was not the best throughout my childhood, I have one thing that I can forever be thankful for: that my mother decided to bring me into this world, which was greatest gift she ever gave me. I will forever be grateful.

It's important for young boys and girls to know that they are not entitled to anything. That time, love and effort their parents give to them is a blessing, and for this they should be grateful. For this, they should always honor their mothers, and a child should be very ashamed to disrespect his or her mother. For this, the answer should change from "I don't want to do it," or "Why?" or "No," to "Yes, Mom," and "I will do it, Mom!"

I know my childhood was not all full of love like I wished, but I still considered myself very blessed. I still obeyed and loved my father, I still bragged about my father to other children. My father was still my hero. And any opportunity I got to be with my hero I took with open arms. Sometimes I felt like I was a burden to him, like I was not the child he wanted, but still I was glad I had someone to call father.

There are a lot of children who grow up without that father figure in their lives. The gangs and pimps become the father figures. There are kids who never get to hear the words he is *just like his father* because the father is not there. There are kids out there who have zero stories to tell about a father. Maybe that father did the easy job of making a woman pregnant and ran away from the hard task of raising a child. Maybe the father is dead or in prison, but the truth is there is no father figure in these kids' lives. A father's influence in his daughter's life shapes her self-esteem, self-image, confidence and opinions of men. But some young girls never have that opportunity to spend time with a father.

I remember, when it would rain, my father would put on his gumboots in the morning and walk out. I would walk behind him following in his footsteps. I tried to fit my little foot in that big footprint father left behind. I liked to imitate my father. My father drank a specific kind of soda—it was a bitter lemon flavor, so I started to drink that too. I actually hated the taste of it, but it made me proud to imitate him. He liked to bite on the end of his collar, and it was not too long before I started to do that. I started to walk like him, talk like him and I took so much pride when people looked at me and said, "He is just like his father." Sadly, not all kids have a father figure to imitate like I did.

Sure I could have used hugs, and I would have appreciated at least one I love you from my parents, but even if it did not go as I would have loved, I am still grateful that I at least had those people to call father and mother. I am glad that they attached some value to me, to put me through school, to give me shelter, put food on my table, give me clothes to wear, and take me to the hospital when I was sick.

In my childhood story, there is much to be justifiably angry about in it, but there is also a lot about which to be happy. I have a lot for which to be grateful. Many things went wrong, but a lot of things did go right. I did not have it all, but I was blessed to have some. And for this I have my dear parents to thank. I love and owe them a whole lot for giving me such a childhood.

I heard a story of a young boy whose dad told him to plough the grounds while he went away to attend to some issues. The young boy said, "Yes, Dad I will do it." Later in the evening when the dad returned home he realized that the boy had ploughed much more than he had asked his son to plough. The father asked the young boy, "Son, I told to only plough this much. Why did you go that far?" The son answered him, "Dad I ploughed this part because you asked me to plough, but when I finished the ground you asked me to plough, I ploughed more just because I love and appreciate you." This father was glad to hear this as I expect many parents would be. It will mean a lot to our parents for us to call them not to ask for anything, or whine about anything but just to say, "Mom and Dad I am grateful for you and I love you."

If I had a choice for parents, I would have chosen those very caring Korean moms, or the loving American missionary couple. But I had no vote in it. Your parents might not be the best, but when God decided to give us the gift of life, He chose our parents. And the same God commands us to "honor your father and your mother, that your days may be long in the land that the Lord your God is giving you" (Exodus 20:12). This is the first commandment given with a promise.

The word honor can also mean not taking your mother and father lightly. By honoring we are called to respect them, fear them, obey them, appreciate them, and be kind to them. The Bible does not say honor your father and mother when they are good to you. Or when they let you do whatever you want to do and buy you whatever you want. The Bible commands us to honor our parents regardless.

To me one of the biggest manifestations of how evil we have become as a society, can be seen by how much children are disobeying their parents. It is a very ugly act when a teenager starts cursing at his or her parents. Yet many children have embraced this ugly evil; an example of this is manifested in the "yo mama" insults that we embrace as jokes. This is taking our mothers lightly. This is not funny, and I think it's rude and very disrespectful. Disrespecting someone's mother in that manner in Uganda could easily get you killed. Mothers are our creators here on earth, and we ought to revere them.

You might say that I really do not know how bad your parents are. Even in that situation, you must honor their position as parents. Not everyone likes Obama as the president of the USA, but they must honor his office. It is easy to honor good and loving parents, but how do we honor those parents that do not act like they love us? What about the abusive parents who treat us like animals? Since the Bible says honor parents, we must honor them too; so we can honor our parents by not returning evil for evil. If they curse at us the honorable thing is to bless them and not curse back. We honor them by praying to God to save them. We leave them in God's hands because He can do a far better job than us. And we honor them by appreciating the fact that, whatever happens, they are our parents. Those parents are far from perfect, but they are the most precious gift God gives to us children.

Like I mentioned above, children do not choose their parents, in the same way parents do not choose who their children are going to be. God does the choosing, and He chooses a mother and father to bring that specific child into the world for a reason. It might not be the kid next door who gets straight A's or that kid who plays piano the best. But it is the child God gave you, and the Bible says children are a blessing from God. So parents, when God reached into His blessing box, He saw it fit to give you that child. That child might not be the best athlete, but he or she is the best blessing God could give you. So parents need to cherish these blessings, and the children in turn should honor the parents.

When I watch parents who do not seem to treasure the blessing of having children, I wonder if they are doing what my parents did. Instead of loving children they just tolerate them, and deny them the opportunity of really enjoying parental love. Statistics show that in America every 26 seconds a child runs away from home. Could this be because they are rebellious children or because the parents are unloving? As a believer, I find only two things any parent must do for their children. Love them and lead them to Christ.

Billy Graham once said, "Children will invariably talk, eat, walk, think, respond, and act like their parents. Give them a target to shoot at. Give them a goal to work toward. Give them a pattern that they can see clearly, and you give them something that gold and silver cannot buy." What have you given your children? Give them criticism and they will learn to condemn. Give them hate and they will learn to fight and hate. Give them ridicule and they will be shy. Give them encouragement and they will be confident. Give them love and they will learn to love. Give them security and they will learn to have faith. And most importantly, give them the Word of God and they will learn to lead a Godly life.

Deuteronomy 6:6-8 says, "And these words that I command you today shall be on your hear. You shall teach them diligently to your children, and shall talk of them when you sit in your house, and when you walk by the way, and when you lie down, and when you rise. You shall bind them as a sign on your hand, and they shall be as frontlets between your eyes.

The first thing that jumps right off the page in verse 7 is that we need to make time to be with the children, because we cannot teach them these commandments unless we spend time with them, whether sitting at home or hanging out outside home. The emphasis is not teaching them but sitting with them or spending time with them. The text does not say sit down and teach them. The teaching them only came because the parent was sitting down with the children. The verse is talking about the non-violent violence of neglect that many children suffer. This violence has pushed kids to spend more time on the streets than at home.

When parents only spend limited time with their children, it is hard to teach the children anything. The only time children have their parent's attention is when they walk in with a bruise on his head, a broken arm, or a bloody shirt. Often parents assume everything is okay with their children if they don't see any obvious injuries. However, bruises on the heart, broken dreams, and low self-esteem which many children suffer every day go unnoticed. Parents would have known such things if they spent quality time with their children. There are times when the mom and dad just have to be there for the kids, such as school presentations, birthday parties, bedtime stories, and more. I really needed my parents to come through on visitation days when I was in boarding school.

O. A. Battista said, "The best inheritance a parent can give his children is a few minutes of his time each day."

The next point from the passage is that we have to lead by example. Sometimes parents think they can just give orders and say, "Do as I say, not as I do." But that is wrong. Children watch their parents, examine their morals, watch their actions and try to do as mom and dad do, not so much as they say.

"It's not only children who grow," said Joyce Maynard. "Parents do too. As much as we watch to see what our children do with their lives, they are watching us to see what we do with ours. I can't tell my children to reach for the sun. All I can do is reach for it myself."

Because our actions speak louder than words, when we teach children God's values and commandments, we have to apply those same values and commandments to ourselves too or our efforts will be a total joke. You can teach kids to love, but if nothing you do shows love, these kids will not know what love looks like. Whatever a parent tells their children is all talk. It only becomes a teaching or lesson when the kids see their parents walk their talk.

I have heard parents say that they are bad parents because they had bad parents, so they do not know a better way to do things. In Uganda we had sports days at school, and one of the most interesting sports for me was running. On one rainy day, the athletes lined up for baton relay, but somehow one of the batons dropped on the ground and got dirty. So everyone that ran that race was passed a dirty baton, and they ran with a dirty baton. After that round, though, someone did not like the dirty baton and cleaned it. And when the second round came, the same baton was being passed, but this time it was a clean baton. It is true that many fathers have passed a dirty baton down to their children, and as the children go, they just pass the same dirty baton down to their children. This forms a cycle of the dirty baton. But someone has to realize that this is a dirty baton, someone has to desire for a change, and someone has to clean the baton. I do not feel like my father passed me a clean baton, but if God gives me the opportunity to have children, it is a great privilege to correct the mistakes my father made by passing my kids a clean baton. We might have never had perfect parents, and we are not perfect, but we all have a chance to mold our children.

Parents have a God-given opportunity to shape their kids to be children after God's own heart, to be responsible citizens and to be the best they can be. But if we do not take that opportunity, the world (gangs, pimps, TV, etc.) will gladly take over teaching our kids. The world will teach them how to talk dirty, how to use their bodies to get what they want, how to fight and do all sorts of evil. But that is a very dangerous road to take, and God did not design it like that. He designed this teaching to happen at home. Parents and children, God has a greater purpose and desires for our specific families. It is my prayer that children will honor parents and that parents will lead their children in a Godly way.

CHAPTER 4

TEENAGE LIFE/ A REWRITTEN JOURNEY

Teenage life was the best and worst point of my life. As a teenager I became really close to my father. He made so much effort to get close to me and spend more time with me. But this was also because he was proud of the progress I was making in my Muslim faith. Of all his many children, he invested in me the most financially and I was his favorite one. Not only was I a favorite to my father but also to relatives and friends who were proud to see me progress in my faith as a Muslim.

In the past our great-grandparents were devout Muslims. They played their part in serving Allah faithfully and they passed the torch down to our parents. So it was our parents' turn to pass the religion down to our generation, to mold us into a generation that would stand for and be faithful to Allah. So any progress we made was met with great joy from our elders. As a boy in the home, there were far more expectations for me than for all my sisters. The most important was to carry on the religion of Islam and make my family proud.

My tremendous progress in the faith gave my family something to brag about to other parents and friends. I spent more time at the mosque than any of my siblings. My uncles and aunties looked at the kids in our family and they considered me to be the best. One of my aunts was a very strict Muslim. None of the kids liked her because they all thought she was scary and mean. On the other hand, I enjoyed spending time her. I thought she was tender and loving. I never understood why my sisters thought she was mean. During the holy month of Ramadan my favorite place to break the fasting each day was at her house. Maybe she was actually mean to my sisters and nice to me, but this was only because I was making an effort to be a better Muslim.

I thought myself somehow different from the other kids around me as early as kindergarten, even with other people in my community but my faith in Allah created a bridge between me my community better. I started to bond well with other Muslim boys and together we hated the non-Muslims, or the infidels. When we played soccer with non-Muslim boys, it always ended in fights. We Muslim boys put aside our differences and bonded on the fact that we all believed in Allah. We walked to mosque in groups, and we stuck together, especially during Ramadan. When people in my community saw me, even elders, they always greeted me in the name of Allah. Things were going really well.

As a reward for my faith in Allah, Father sent me to the top Muslim institute in Uganda. It was the most expensive school anyone in my family had ever attended, and it was a long way from my home. The name of this school was Bilal Muslim Institute. There I was to be groomed to be a better and more devout Muslim. My father and my community at large saw the potential in me to become a great sheikh. This is why they justified investing in me to go four hours away from home to this expensive Muslim school. My father could now meet with other Muslim men and brag about his son attending the best Muslim institute in Uganda. If there was any time I ever truly felt love from my dad, this was it. I was seeing a side of my father that I had not seen before. He spent time with me, he showed me off to his friends, and I could see in his eyes that he was proud of me. This was the best I had it, and I knew that all I had to do was work hard in school and become a better follower of Allah to maintain this love.

Opening day of the new semester my father and I took a four hour drive to Bilal Islamic Institute. Just father and son in the car was special to me. My father and I were doing great, I was getting into the best Muslim school, and hoping to graduate from this school as the best Muslim I could be.

There was nothing more I could ask for in life. We finally got to the school campus. It was huge. The mosque was gigantic and the atmosphere so felt different. Everyone looked too serious, and it scared me a little bit, but I did not want to show my father any kind of fear. We unloaded my luggage from the car, and I had to say goodbye to my father.

As a few days past I discovered quickly that this was indeed the strictest Muslim environment I had ever been in. Prayers five times a day were compulsory and I had to be at the mosque on time. Failure to do so or acting lazy, especially for the morning prayers, meant I got a serious whooping. If the teachers did not cane me, other student leaders did. The mission was to create a more devout and strong Muslim out of me, and whatever needed to be done for me to get there was done. After a few beatings, I shaped up, and I was never again late for prayers or the Quran lessons.

I learnt so much about the Muslim religions from attending prayers every day, listening to the Imam teach and reading the Quran myself. We had to study and memorize Quran chapters with a goal of memorizing the entire Quran during a given period of time. If you failed to memorize you were punished by caning. Putting someone in pain was the best form of punishment. To avoid the punishments I worked hard to memorize chapters in the Quran, and I successfully memorized several of them. In a few months I was able to sing out different chapters from the Quran.

I could not wait to go back home on vacations to recite them for my family and friends who had so much faith in me. I wanted to show the entire village how much I had learnt. I was very proud of how much knowledge I had gained. I thought to myself, *if these people loved me before I joined the Bilal Islamic Institute, when I literally knew nothing about Islam, now that I have actually learnt a lot and can recite chapters in the Quran, these people will worship me.*

I was now officially a sheikh because of the knowledge I had acquired at Bilal. It was such a great achievement for a boy like me. I was soon going to start teaching my sisters the religion as well as some kids around the village. I thought to myself now I stood the chance to be among Muslim leaders in my community. I was by far the leader in the family at that point. I remember one time we had an event at my grandfather's house, and just to show off I spoke Arabic before everyone. I had never seen grandpa so proud of me like he was at that moment. This was the best time because I felt love from all corners from my Muslim community.

Love always got the best out of me. I tried to work had as a Muslim because of the love I was receiving. I loved my friend Peace; that's why I fought for her. I loved my animals; that is why I worked so hard to feed them in the bush. I was driven by love. And without love I felt like my tank became empty, like it had at the boarding school. I became a different, unpleasant person. And for some reason I felt very little love for or from my new school Bilal Muslim Institute.

Strangely I was different from the other students at school, for starters I was one of the smallest students, if not the smallest, on campus. In my actions I was different. I was very bothered with the punishments administered to other students. I was unsettled by the idea of Jihad, because to me Jihad does not represent love in anyway. My conversations were different; I preferred to tell jokes and making people laugh. I shied away from fights; I smiled way too much. When I talked many thought that I sounded like a child. I was given the nickname "baby." For the longest time everyone on campus called me baby so that eventually most students even forgot my real name.

Babies and grownups have very few things in common. I was the baby and everyone else was grown. I started feeling like I was in the wrong place. I did not belong there. This school was for young warriors ready to fight for Islam, but I was a soft baby. I was almost ashamed to go back to my village where people were proud of me as a new sheikh. Yet at the school I was the least, the baby. I felt like I was a joke, and my father was wasting a lot money on me.

Back in my village I was something, but at school I was nothing. My pride told me I could work hard and be tough, bold and diligent like students. I trained myself not to care about certain things that would have bothered me. I trained myself to hate infidels and to defend the religion like other students. It was hard at first because that was not what I really wanted, but the longer I did it the easier it became. I tried so hard to change my identity from "baby" to something like "sheikh" or "Mohammed Ali." I became meaner and, started to show no love for infidels. My speech started changing, and sure enough, one day someone said, "You are no baby. You're bad." It was meant to insult me, instead it edified me. I'd been trying so hard not to be a baby and now it was paying off.

I was slowly gaining momentum at being a radical, but the more I studied the Muslim religion, the more I came across things that confused me. Some things made me wonder and question our most common everyday practices—sometimes things just did not add up at all. I felt bad at this point, because I was just making the transition from "baby" to "sheikh" but now I was failing to understand what the Quran was saying to me. And worse of all, doubt began to creep into my heart. I felt like I was the most horrible Muslim student ever. So I had to rid myself of the doubts and believe in my religion, in the true prophet Mohammed and in Allah.

When you do something wrong for too long, sometimes it starts to feel right. In my heart, I knew my meanness toward non-Muslims was wrong, but after time it started to feel right. I was a part of the group of young men who caused chaos and threw stones at some Christian crusades in my village. At the time, in the group, it felt good and right. But when I was all alone there was a very small voice in my head telling me this was wrong. So a part of me felt disgusted with my actions. But unfortunately, the radical me received more praise, had more friends and was accepted by many. So it was easy to ignore that small voice.

Ignoring something does not necessarily mean it will go away. That voice stuck with me, it always made me feel like I was wrong and on the wrong path. One of the most painful things to do is to try to be something you are not and live the life that was not meant for you to live. I was trying to live the life of my Muslim friends at school or the Muslims I saw on TV. I was walking on the path that was not set for me, so I was going the wrong direction because I was following others. Sometimes we wonder why we get lost in life. Things are not working out but we forget that we are on the wrong path. God set a different path for us but we chose to follow people.

I followed people, because that is what the Muslim religion is really about. We are Muslims not because we chose to, but because our parents and their parents were Muslims. So I followed them, and they were happy with my progress. I also seemed happy in the crowd. But when I was all alone without my Muslim friends, I was sad. I felt like I was in bondage and was not peaceful. The smiles and laughs I had with my friends turned into tears when I was all alone. I seemed happy on the outside, but deep within I was miserable. My main aim became to please my Muslim crowd, at the expense of my joy.

I was getting so used to making my Muslim family happy that, it no longer mattered how miserable I was. I was giving up the life God meant for me to live, and taking up the life they wanted me to live. However for some reason my father was running low on funds, and he could not afford the expensive Islamic institute anymore. So he decided to transfer me from Bilal Islamic Institute to a cheaper school. I was very excited to get this news, because I craved a change. I did not belong at Bilal. Thank God for the financial hardship my father went through that made it possible for me to get out of Bilal before I became a totally different person.

CHAPTER 5

NEW SCHOOL/ NEW LIFE STYLE

The search was on for a new school, I was only hoping the new school would be nothing like Bilal. To my surprise it was not another Muslim institute. It was a non-denominational school, though it was mostly Catholic. I could take this school over any of the Muslim institutes out there. Even though I only changed schools, this transition also changed my life. I was not under as much pressure to live a certain lifestyle. I felt a sense of relief from all the Quran memorization, morning prayers and the harsh punishments.

The pressure to follow other people and make them happy was lifted, however, the change left me very worried about my faith. In Uganda we say to keep a single coal burning it must burn together with other coals; if you separate one piece of coal from the rest, that one piece will burn out. Muslim friends thought I would burn out. But I assured everyone not to worry because I thought I would find other Muslim boys at this new school, and we would keep burning together. And some people in my village felt that I had too much fire for the Muslim faith to burn out. I really felt like the separated piece of coal, because there were very few Muslim students at the school. And of these few, most were not devout.

The separation, though it seemed to shut out all the voices from my Muslim friends, magnified that small voice that always told me I was on the wrong path. This voice was getting clearer, and my small doubts about the Islamic faith were growing. I did not want to doubt my faith. I wanted to be a true worshipper of Allah, so I deemed this voice to be evil, and I tried all I could to get it out of my head. It felt bad, because I was fighting this voice alone. If I had my friends from Bilal I would have easily shut out the voice. But I was separated from them, on an island by myself.

Years later I look back and I know God orchestrated the move to this new school just to get me away from all my peers and the voices that were crowding my head. God sent me to this island so that I could begin to hear His voice and listen to Him rather than my friends' voices. He was that small voice, and He wanted me to hear Him loud and clear. I think, when God speaks, He's always loud and clear. We just can't hear Him because we have all these other voices in our heads overshadowing God's voice. That is why many times God has to get us alone.

"Jacob was left alone; and there wrestled a man (God) with him until the breaking of the day" (Genesis 32:24). Isolation is the forerunner of revelation, grace, salvation, and blessing. God has a purpose for getting us alone because it is when we are alone that we can hear, see and feel God without distraction. Paul, on the road to Damascus, was separated from his companions by a light from heaven and this was when Paul became a follower of Christ. The woman that was caught in adultery was left alone with Jesus, and that was when she received forgiveness and salvation. There is purpose in God's separation.

God was setting me alone so that I could see Him, but like Jacob I was wrestling, though I was wrestling against being alone with God. Time alone with God was making me see that I was following a lie, that I was not really worshipping the only true God as a Muslim. When we are left alone with God that is the only time we come to realize how corrupt we are, how sinful we are, and how lost we are. I was fighting this because I never wanted to believe or see how wrong I was. I was trained all my life to believe in Allah and I was not about to let some voice to tell me otherwise.

Therefore I kept resisting, I convinced myself that new school was affecting me the wrong way. With time I would get back to myself. I even talked to someone about these things, his response was that I "should never doubt Allah or his holy prophet Mohammed." That was worst sin. I tried different things to block out this voice: I got a girlfriend, made new friends, got into sports, and started dancing. However none of all these things could block out that voice.

That voice seemed like a bad thing, but the crazy part was that most of the stuff it said made perfect sense. Sometimes truth is the hardest thing to face. The voice in my head right; Jihad made no sense, and I knew it was right because I felt the same way. The voice was right; the idea of dying in Jihad (killing, which is evil) and going straight to heaven, where virgins would be waiting for you, made little sense. The voice was right; God was big enough to defend Himself. I did not need to fight and kill people to defend Allah. It was right to be driven by love not hate. If it only came down to the fact that all I needed was to fight other people to protect my faith, I would have been disqualified, because I was just not a fighter. I was called a baby for crying out loud. Fighting needs warriors, not soft babies. The voice made sense, but it was not about what made sense, it was about what I desired to do, which was to follow the religion of my family.

This voice created a hunger in me to find answers to the doubts it had placed in my head. I thought digging deeper to find out more about my faith would help. However, this created more doubts. A wise man told me never to ask questions for which I was not ready to get answers. I was asking those questions in my quest for answers. I learnt that all Muslims face Mecca while praying, but when they get to Mecca the face a black box called the Kaaba. During prayers we got down on our knee, and put our head on the floor which to me is a posture of worship. But the same Quran teaches that God is in heaven, and He is everywhere. Could it be that maybe we were bowing and worshipping the Kaaba in Mecca? If God was everywhere, then we could face any direction and worship Him. Was my worship going to God or to Mecca?

I had questions like these that seemed to come in like a flood, but worse than that, I could not really find answers to these questions. This was the first time I really questioned God and my worship, where it was just my relationship with Him. I had been so busy with all the other rules that I never really focused to me and God. I think that might be the one of the problems with religions; they have too many practices that keep us occupied thus distracting us from really focusing and knowing God. Such Muslim practices include pilgrimages to Mecca, dressing up a certain way, washing a certain way, memorizing the Quran, fighting infidels, going to the mosque five times a day, eating and not eating certain food, observing Ramadan and more. There is so much focus on these practices and less focus on my relationship with God.

Changing one's belief might be the hardest thing to do; even though all these things did not make sense, I stood firm in my faith as a Muslim. Islam was all I knew, it was in my family, in my lifestyle, in the way I thought and viewed the world. I did not need any reason to believe in Allah, it became something I did unconsciously. And if I listened to the voice and changed my beliefs, it would mean that I was wrong all my life. It would mean my father, my relatives, my role models, and all my teachers were wrong because they all believed in Allah. I knew people who memorized the entire Quran; there was no way they were wrong. But later I found out that wrong is wrong regardless of how many people think otherwise.

I kept fighting, I kept standing, and I tried even harder to block that voice out. I became a crazy boy on campus, everyone knew who I was. I started running around with ill-mannered boys, chasing girls and just having a good time through high school. This behavior, by the way, got me kicked out of school later. I started watching the English Premiere League and I got hooked on this. My favorite team was and still is Arsenal. However all these things were temporary solutions, but they never really satisfied the thirst that voice had created in me. The Bible says, "*Today, when you hear his voice, don't harden your hearts as Israel did when they rebelled*" (*Hebrews 3:15*). I heard God's voice but I was doing the exact opposite of what He was saying.

I was kicked out of school, and I went home expecting my mother to kill me. But when I got home she was a different person. My mother told me that she had heard a voice, and she decided to become a Christian. I was upset thinking maybe it was the same voice I was hearing. This voice had misled my mother, but I was ready to stand strong and battle with it. My mother's change got a bad reception from my father and the rest of the family. I was upset too, so I sided with my father against her. I spoke ill about her to my father. She had another son before she met my father, so I told him that all she really cared about was her first son, not us. I would tell my grandmother that it was a mistake for my father to marry her because there is no way I would marry a woman with a child. What I told my father made him very angry, so much so that he went on to tell his mother. This stirred up hatred for my mother in the family. I hate talking about this part, because I am not proud of it. What I did still bothers me.

Despite all I did she prayed for me and got me into a new school. At this new school closer to home, I would spend the weekdays at school and come back home over the weekends. However, one Saturday I came back home and the house looked different. Some things were missing, and my mother was not there. I found out that mom was gone, and there was violence involved because she was a Christian. If there is one time that I have been the angriest in my life this was the time—the thought of someone laying hands on my mother woke up hatred in my heart that I didn't even know I had. I was also angry because I played a part in it, with all the ill-talking and lies I told about my mom.

My heart was crushed. Home did not feel like home anymore. I remember walking through the streets and weeping. Though I tried to hold it back I could not. People saw me and asked what the problem was and I told them my mother was gone. Part of my weeping was anger that she was kicked out and for the way it happened. But I also wept with regret that I was not a good son, wishing I had just one day to put everything right with my mother. I would have never talked ill about her. I did not know how much I loved her, and how important she was in the home until I came back home and she was not there anymore. I was very angry with myself. I learnt the hard way how not to take mothers for granted when we have them. Because a time might come when we will not have them anymore.

Washington Irving said that,

> A mother is the truest friend we have, when trials heavy and sudden fall upon us; when adversity takes the place of prosperity; when friends desert us; when trouble thickens around us, still will she cling to us, and endeavor by her kind precepts and counsels to dissipate the clouds of darkness, and cause peace to return to our hearts.

The next day my father met me and he was very disappointed that I was crying over my mother—even my grandmother was very disappointed. I guess they thought that I was going to celebrate, but instead I was hurt. It is that hard time that truly opened my eyes to the violence I was trying to embrace. This radicalism had happened to my own mother. I despise violence to this day. It makes me sick to hear of men beating their wives. I despise any idea of Jihad or fighting in the name of religion. It is evil from the pits of hell.

This happened shortly after the 911 attack on America by Osama Bin Laden. I remembered some of my young Muslim friends rejoicing. Bin Laden became a hero to them, some even nicknamed themselves Bin Laden. Originally, it seemed like a good thing, but after violence happened in my home I was completely sickened by what happened in America. My friends looked like total idiots to celebrate violence. Violence in homes, and in the community is very evil. There is nothing to justify it. It breaks relationships, takes lives and cause pain. God hates violence, and if we embrace violence we embrace evil, not God.

Someone I respected so much had embraced evil that he was willing to hurt my mom for the cause of religion. However this was when I asked myself the big question. Why?? Why should I embrace evil? Why should I continue holding on to things that do not make sense? Why do I have to follow the religion I doubt so much? I feel like this is an important place to get to in life, when we ask why. Why am I here? Why am I doing this and that? Why? I asked why, and the only answer that I came up with was because I was told to do so, and not because I chose to do so.

It was ok to stay at home because my father told me so, but it was a totally different story for me to let him decide my relationship with God. That was not good enough, so I decided to stop blocking that voice in my head. I decided to pay attention. When I did pay attention there was a heavy thirst in my heart, for an answer to all the questions that were in my head. This thirst was stronger than thirst for water after playing basketball. It was deeper than that.

David wrote, *"As the deer pants for the water brooks, so pants my soul for You, O God" (Psalm 42).*

I liked to be out in the bush with the animals. There are some dry places in my country; places where there was a volcanic eruption back in the day and the lava now covers streams of water. When animals move from one place to another looking for water they reach this place covered with lava or a rock. As they walk by they can smell the water under that rock. I imagine their expectations to finally get to some cold spring even heighten their thirst. They try to scratch the rock away to get to that water they can smell. They scratch and pound the rock till their hoofs start bleeding, their legs get tired and weak, their energy dissipates and they give up. The thirst is too much. The animals try everything possible to get to that water. In the same way I was thirsty but like those animal I was looking for water in the wrong place. I was searching the Quran, Mosque or Muslim friends. Like the animals, I felt if I tried harder I would find my answers, but it never worked.

However there is a place I could find answers. There was a place the animals could find water without having to expend so much energy. The streams flowed under a rock, but they flowed into a well not too far away. If the animals could just get to this well, they could drink to the fill. There was one place I had to look to quench my thirst. That was the real God.

CHAPTER 6

QUEST FOR ANSWERS

Did answers actually exist for my numerous questions about God? If they did exist, where were they? Who had these answers? These were the questions that went through my head as I began a quest for answers. I started reading a little bit about other religions, but stuff did not really make sense to me. I was failing early on and I desired to know how I was going to find my answers. I figured I needed to talk to people from these other religions, so they can tell me about their beliefs. But most of the people I knew, we had gotten into fights over religion. And since I was still a Muslim, I was not just going to just start telling non-Muslims I had doubts over my religion.

One morning I walked around like I had a GPS in my head telling me specifically where to go. I listened and went. The final destination was a café called Source at about 11 AM This café is frequented by foreigners who go there to use the internet, hangout, shop or buy food. As I walked by the Source café that morning, I saw three American men hanging out at the patio. They were playing a card game called UNO, so I thought they might be working for United Nations Organization. However, one of them, Patrick Atkins, was wearing a cross, and right at that moment I felt the need to go talk to these "Mzungu" ... that is Swahili for "white people."

It was just three of them, but there were four seats. I was scared but for some reason I felt like these men could have some answers for my questions about God. My thirst was too much, that fear could not stand in my way.

So I walked closer to them, and asked whether I could take the fourth seat and play the card game with them. When I asked, it seemed like they were waiting for a fourth person to show up and it was me. With open arms they welcomed me to play with them. Patrick, who was eating a chapatti, offered me some of it. People who know me will be surprised to hear this, but I said, "No thank you."

Overall these three young men Jacob Via, Jared Via and Patrick seemed like very nice people. They taught me how to play the game, which was quite fun. Also they did not work for United Nations Organization. UNO was just the name of the card game. It was so much fun. I actually won a game. Anyway, I had an agenda to find answers. I just did not know how to make a good transition from having fun to asking serious question.

However, I was given the green light when they told me that they were in Uganda for a mission trip. This opened a way for me to ask them about their God, but I did it in a different way. I started a debate with them about Islam and Christianity. I still had some pride as a Muslim. I wouldn't just go out and tell them Islam didn't make sense anymore. However they did not debate with me. They just told me what they knew was right and backed it up with the Bible, so it was not just their words. Most of my beliefs had no backing except others peoples' words and actions.

One thing that hit home that morning was what they called God's love for me. This love drove God to send His only son to die on the cross for my sins so that I could have a relationship with God. I feel like sometimes people speak either to the heart or to the ears. Whatever is spoken to the ears goes right in one ear and out the other, but whatever is spoken to the heart sticks within us. That day when those young men talked about God's love for me, they spoke to my heart. This God seemed different from Allah.

Thinking about this God's love for me, I was left amazed. We eventually parted ways but I was still meditating on this loving God. I was driven by love to fight the kindergarten Goliath, Asheraf, when he messed with Peace, so it made sense to me that this God could be driven by love to save us. But what never made sense is how far God went to save us—He gave His only Son! Imagine a father had four bad kids, a thief, a murderer, a rapist, and a liar. A rich man comes and asks this man if he can buy one of the kids. Not to kill them but care for them. I think any loving father will say, "No thank you, keep your money. My children are not for sale." Yet God gave a perfect son to be killed. That is crazy love!

That is the love that got me thinking seriously about this God, loving and being loved was all I wanted since I was a small boy. Love is what got the best out of me. After I heard about God's love for me from these boys, I knew that no love I could ever get in this world even comes close to God's love for me. When men sinned, God could have easily called a Jihad against us all, but instead He gave us love.

So if Allah and Prophet Mohammed really do embrace Jihad, then according to my comparisons they were very different from this God. Different in a negative way. Jesus was beaten, ridiculed, falsely accused and killed on the cross, yet He never called a Jihad on His accusers. I thought there must be something about this man, Jesus Christ. He went through all He experienced because of love. And what was really special was when the young men were talking to me, they made it seem very personal to me. That Jesus died for ME, so even if I was the only one, Christ would have still died for. He loved ME.

There was something about this man Jesus Christ that caught my attention, I wanted to know more about Him, that day I did not give my life to Christ but I told the young men that I would be glad to talk about Christ again with them. And Jared promised to bring me a Bible the next time so that I can find out these things on my own. He wanted to show me that all the things they told me were not their words but the very Word of God.

Sure enough the next day, we met up, and Jared had a Bible for me. That was the first and probably the best gift he ever gave me. They invited me to hang out with them the rest of the day. We went out to a village to build a platform for a crusade that the rest of the team was going to use when they got to Uganda. The three young men came ahead to prepare for a big group of people that was coming for a short mission trip in Uganda. It was a long ride. I asked a lot of questions about Christ, and when I went back home I read my Bible.

Jared had marked out a few pages for me to read in the Bible; it was amazing to find out that I, Emmanuel Nester, could have a relationship with YHWH. It could be just me and God. This was the first time I heard that. Before it was my religion, the practices, the Imam, and all the other things except the most important thing—my relationship with the creator of heaven and earth.

And in this relationship, God would accept me just as I was. I did not have to memorize the Quran. I did not have to make a pilgrimage to Mecca. I did not have to dress a certain way, speak a certain language, or go for prayers five times a day. This relationship did not depend on what I could do, but on what God did. There were no strings attached, all I had to do is accept Jesus Christ into my life—in my quest for answers I felt like this was what I had been looking for all along: Jesus Christ.

But it is not enough just to know where the answer is. Like the thirsty animal I talked about, it would do that animal no good if it walks down to the well but does not stoop down to drink the water and quench its thirst. God offers us the gift of Salvation, but it is not ours until we accept it. I was sure without a shadow of a doubt that Jesus was who I was looking for in my quest for answers. That is why I decided to say, "Yes, Lord, come into my life."

When I invited Him into my life, He came and I felt the change. My thirst was quenched, my quest came to an end, and a heavy burden was lifted off of me. That burden was replaced by some kind of peace that is hard to explain in words. That day I was driven by God's love to the cross of Christ where I laid it all down, in order to follow Christ. I believed He was a better God than Allah, before I gave my life to Christ. And after I gave my life to Christ and felt what was going on inside me, I did not simply believe that He was a better God. I knew that He was the only true God, the God of Abraham, Isaac and Jacob. The great I AM!

It was at that moment that I understood that the small voice I kept hearing was not just a voice or my hallucination but the very voice of God. He was leading me to the cross. Those times I was so disgusted with some of the Muslim practices, it was not me who was really disgusted but God. He orchestrated my move from Bilal. He opened my eyes up to see Him. He put the three missionary boys at the Source café at the right time, for me to meet them. He ordered my steps to the cross, and when I got there it all made sense.

I remember telling Jared that I wish I had become a Christian earlier, I felt like I had wasted fourteen years of my life following a lie instead of following YHWH. But all these times God was calling me, I chose to harden my heart and resist Him. The Bible says that God stands out and knocks. If we open the door and let Him in, He will come. God had been knocking on my door for a long time. And for a long time I locked Him out, but He kept knocking. Today everyone who still has breath has the same opportunity that I had to open their doors and let God in.

I was now a new believer in Christ. However the boys told me that was not the end of the story, but the first step. The next step was to become a disciple. The first call is *"come unto me" (Matthew 11:28),* but the next call is *"come after me" (Matthew 16:24).* I had answered the call to follow Christ like the twelve men did in the Bible, but they answered that second call and they were now referred to as disciples not just followers or believers. A disciple and a believer are different. However, Christ has called us to make disciples, *"Go therefore and make disciples of all nations, baptizing them in the name of the Father and of the Son and of the Holy Spirit," (Matthew 28:19).*

As a believer I received the gift of eternal life through Jesus Christ. Now as a disciple I had to dedicate my life to Jesus Christ daily. Discipleship was not going to be a onetime decision like believing and receiving salvation. It was going to be the rest of my life. *"So Jesus said to the Jews who had believed him, "If you abide in my word, you are truly my disciples, 32 and you will know the truth, and the truth will set you free." (John 8:31-32).*

The three boys wanted me not to be a mere believer in Christ but a disciple of Christ, and the first thing I needed to do was to get into a church that preached God's word. This was emphasized because there are a lot of churches preaching a manmade Gospel, not the one Christ preached. This was also to help me be in fellowship with other believers. Then I needed to get grounded in God's word, because as a disciple, God's word is the lamp unto my feet. Without it I stumble. I needed to hide God's word in my heart that I would not sin against Him. Coupled with this, I needed to pray always, not just to ask God for stuff but to talk to my heavenly Father. And finally I needed to go out and make other disciples.

CHAPTER 7

DISCIPLESHIP

Answering the call to salvation is like laying the firm foundation of a house, and answering the call to discipleship is like building on the foundation until it is a beautiful house at the end of the day. So I started out by going to church with the three boys, praying, reading my Bible and sharing my faith. I will start with the last one—sharing my faith.

About seven days after I met Jared, Patrick and Jacob, the rest of Rick Via team jetted into the country for their annual Uganda mission trip. I was invited me to meet the rest of the team once they had rested up after the long flight from America. Jared introduced me to his father and mother who were the team leaders. Also on the team were his brothers Joshua and Jonathan and his sister Joy. Of course I had already met Jacob, so the entire family was in Uganda to share their faith in Christ. Jared told them about my salvation, and everyone seemed to welcome me in very well.

Because these people came a long way to share their faith, I figured it would be a good opportunity for me to also share my faith. So after they had rested up the first day, they started ministry the next morning. The team brought medical supplies; they treated people and shared the gospel in the rural villages of Eastern Uganda. At the first village I mainly translated for Jared as he shared. I spoke three different languages so I was able to translate for most of the people that came. It was fun and I was really excited because at times he would just let me share my story with the Muslims that showed up

Translating was not as easy when some team members spoke. The English they spoke was a bit different from the English I knew. One time someone opened up with "Howdy y'all?" The Ugandan people were waiting for me to translate, and I was looking to him thinking, Would you please speak English! He was looking at me with a smile on his face waiting for me to translate. Another time I had to translate to a kid that she was "cute as a button." In Lugandan, "cute as a button" might be offensive. I do not know about American buttons, but there was nothing cute about the buttons in Uganda.

About two hours after we started, suddenly I started feeling very sick. I ran a fever and had very severe headache. Regardless of how much I wanted to be out there with the team doing evangelism, my body would not let me. I was really upset, because I was very excited to share about how Christ is real and how He had changed my life. I wanted to let people know that I was convinced beyond all doubt that Christ was the Son of God, who died on the cross for our sins and He was the only way to God. It was my deepest desire for my fellow Ugandans to come to Christ's saving knowledge and to have the joy and peace that come with it.

I asked God to bring immediate healing so that I could go be a witness for Him. I was not healed as quickly as I wanted, so I missed out on the whole day. In the bus, a very loving lady, Debbie Ireson, brought me some medicine to take care of my headache, and after I took my medicine I slept. When I woke up it was about time to go back home, but the good thing was that I was feeling better. I only looked forward to another opportunity to share His love with non-believers the next day.

The next day I was feeling perfectly fine, so I joined up with the team and took off for the next village. I had another opportunity to share my faith with others. My biggest goal was to explain to the Muslims how God opened my eyes and saved me. I had opportunities as we talked to different people who came to get medical help. I found out that most of the Muslims I talked too could neither understand nor read Arabic, therefore they had no idea what the Quran said. They just inherited the religion from their families.

No matter who I was interpreting for that day, I would tell them to close their gospel tracks for a moment and let me share what God was doing in my life when we talked to Muslims. For some Muslims, it took a very long time to understand or believe what I was saying. Some never wanted to listen; as a matter of fact they started hating me the minute they found out that I had changed. Some assumed that the Americans had given me money to change. But also God used me to draw many Muslims to Christ during this time. The missionaries would send the Muslims to me, when they seemed not to understand. God was using my testimony to open the eyes of men.

In sharing my testimony I was obeying the call to be a disciple of my master Jesus Christ. I had a testimony to share, and I believe all believers in Christ have a testimony to share with the world. Those many Muslims needed to hear what God was doing in my life. They needed to hear that I was a new creature in Jesus Christ and my entire slate was wiped clean. They needed to see the joy, peace and freedom that I was living in because I accepted Christ. To me, Islam felt like a prison. I was locked in and I was going to die in that prison, until Christ walked in and set me free. The Muslims heard that and many of them left asking, "What must I do to be saved?"

I was already a person who loved to talk A LOT, but I spent time talking about what other people had done, what my parents had done, the Government, my school. I talked about movies, what Chuck Norris was capable of, sports, music, to mention but a few things. But after I met Jesus Christ, nothing I had ever experienced in my entire life could even come close to what Christ did for me. If anything was worth talking about it was salvation, and if anyone was worth talking about it was Jesus Christ. As a disciple, I wanted to and still want to make His name known all over the world.

"And there is salvation in no one else, for there is no other name under heaven given among men[a] by which we must be saved." (Acts 4:12). No name but the name of Jesus!

As I shared my faith I took another step in discipleship. I began to learn God's word. I read the small Bible I was given often but I did not understand much of it. Therefore I spent loads of time with people on the team asking questions about the Bible and learning more about it. Debbie Ireson, one of the older ladies on the team, spent a great deal of time teaching me about the Bible. Different people on the team took turns spending time talking to me and educating me about the Bible. I enjoyed every moment of it because I was learning a lot.

As God's word made sense to me, it became so exciting to read; have you ever witnessed something so awesome that you just can't wait to tell someone about it? We talk on the phone, write emails and letters, or even travel long distances to go tell people about these awesome things we witnessed. I love sports, especially soccer and basketball. I think LeBron James is the greatest basketball player now. I have spoken in my travels, called, emailed and Facebooked about how great he is. God's word blew me away. It was like fire in my bones, and the more I read it, I just had to talk about it.

I told Jared that I was reading some really cool stuff about God's word, and I desired for the other people to see how awesome the Word was. Jared told Rick, the team leader, and I was given a couple of minutes to share about the Word of God. I took about fourteen minutes, I was nervous, and I lost confidence in my English but this was special and nothing was going to stop me from sharing His word. This was the first time I ever stood before believers to proclaim God's Word. Later that night, Josh told me that it was a good word, except I kept clicking the pen out of nervousness.

I started reading a couple of books, and during that short time we spent together, the team worked hard to have me grounded in God's word. I was told that I needed that the most. It was like driving a car with a map, without which you get lost. Without God's word I was sure to get lost. They told me there are many people who answered the call to salvation but diverted from God's word and are lost. The importance of God's Word was stressed so much that I decided whatever church I go to, it MUST be preaching God's word and not diverting from it.

The next step in discipleship was fellowship, fellowship not only in church but even outside church. I spent some of the best time in my whole life with the Rick Via team. To this point this was the best fellowship I have ever been a part of. They were very loving. The words they said to me were encouraging, and edifying. Every day I looked forward to fellowship with these people. In fellowship we prayed together, sang praises to God together, and ate together. If it was up to me, I would have made all of them stay in Uganda with me.

The only problem was that it was not up to me, these people also were going to leave like Peace left. I was so used to that sweet fellowship that we shared, but I knew that they would be leaving soon, and maybe, like Peace, I would never get to see them again. The time came when I had to say good bye. It was their last night, and they had a party to thank the helpers. As the party went on, I was not concerned about the good food or the gifts that volunteers were going to get, but I was sad that these folks were not going to be in Uganda tomorrow.

My name was called to go up and receive a gift for helping out with the team. I was sitting with Joy Via in the back and I was very sad. I remember people clapping for me as I went up to get my gift, but at that point it was not about the gift, it was about my new friends leaving.

After the gifts were given, the time came when we had to say goodnight and goodbye. Debbie Ireson was the first person I ran to. I hugged her and I would not let go. Then I had to say goodbye to the three young men Jared, Patrick and Jacob. I hugged Patrick and Jacob they told me, "We love you Emma and we will see you again." Then I went to say goodbye to Jared, and I just broke down and cried. Jared was crying too. I told him I wish he did not have to leave me. Somehow I looked at him as my spiritual father, and I really did not know what to do without him around. For myself, I wished for time for him to answer my unending Bible questions, to teach me new things and just be in fellowship with me.

However he had to go back to America, and all I had was the next few minutes with him. I used that time to cry on his shoulder and hug him without letting go. He promised me that he would come back to Uganda again. I trusted him, and that was my only comfort. I do not remember in my life ever crying that much for anything or anyone, this was the very first time. I felt love around these people that I had never felt before, and I loved them more than I ever loved anyone.

The last part they taught me about discipleship was praying, always. We prayed every night and morning together, we always prayed at the mission field. And I grew in a habit of praying to God, before I went to sleep and before I got out of bed. When they left I felt empty; nothing good seemed good anymore. I lied down in my room and cried, no one understood me, and no one knew what was going on with me. But the one thing that really comforted me was prayer. I prayed all the time for them. I could not be in America with them psychically, but our fellowship always went on spiritually through prayer.

Being a disciple of Christ was made easy for me because the people who helped me become a disciple loved me. It was that love coupled with God's love for me that drove me to answer the call to discipleship. When we decide to love we can touch hearts of men in ways nothing else can. These missionaries used love to draw me to the cross and they used love to help make me a disciple of Christ. I can honestly say that it would have been impossible if it was not for love.

CHAPTER 8

CHRISTIAN SON IN A MUSLIM FAMILY

Have you ever had so much fun with your friends that you almost forgot the trouble waiting for you at home?

I have! I had to be home before 7PM but there were many times I was out there with my friends having so much fun that I forgot the 7PM rule. So I always got in a lot of trouble. However all that trouble was nothing compared to the trouble I was about to meet, for the decision I made to follow Christ. It was so much fun, after I became a believer in Christ that I almost forgot I was part of a Muslim family that did not tolerate Christians in the house, like my mother.

Those first days were fun, and I also had a team of people who spent time with me on a daily basis, people who really loved me. This almost made me forget that there are people who might hate me for becoming a believer in Christ. That team of missionaries was no longer in the country and it was all coming back to me. Like the times I played with my friends past 7PM, I clearly remembered my curfew on the way home at 8PM That morning I woke up, stayed home the whole day, none of my Christian friends where there, and that is when I realized trouble might be coming very shortly.

I was very comfortable and confident when the team was in Uganda. I was all for sharing my story with other Muslims, but I had done that in the distant villages we went to for missions. However, when they left the country, my confidence and boldness to share the gospel seemed to leave, too. I was left with fear of how my family would react to me becoming a Christian. And fear about how I was supposed to explain this decision to any of my friends who hated Christians. I had become an infidel—the very kind I hated and fought before. Was I going to get the same treatment now, and if so was I ready for it?

I thought to myself, I am not ready. I was not ready for the shame I was about to cause my family by announcing that I am a Christian. I was not ready to see the disappointment on my father's face that the same boy he had so much hopes for, the same boy he spend loads of money on to be in the best Muslim Institute in the country was not the big sheikh in the village but was now an infidel. I was not ready to be the outcast among my friends. According to the Quran I was supposed to be stoned to death and I was definitely not ready for that!

I was not ready to let my people know about the change that I had made, but I was also not ready to go back to Islam after I had tasted the love of Christ. I was in a predicament. I loved my family and friends, but I loved Jesus Christ my Lord and Savior. I feared my father but I also feared my Father in heaven. It felt like there was no middle line where I could have both, yet I wanted to please both God and my people.

I found a short time solution to please God and my people. I would sneak to church on Sunday morning and come back home later after church. And if my father asks where I had been, I would say I went to play soccer. As a disciple of Christ, I needed to be in a church that taught God's word, and gave me the fellowship I needed with other believers. The problem with African churches, though, was that I needed to dress up for church; I could not wear soccer shorts to church. So my back up story of playing soccer would not make sense since I had never dressed up for soccer before.

Also most of the people that I used to play soccer with were fellow Muslim boys, most of whom, by the way, were at home on Sunday mornings. And you would expect someone who went to play soccer to come home stinky and tired. Despite these concerns I just figured this lie would fly or my dad would not waste time trying to find out whether it was true or not.

Despite the fact that my American friends had left the country, the one thing that I knew for sure was that I was going to follow the Lord no matter what. I was determined to not set foot into the mosque again, but to live a new life that reflected my Lord and Savior Jesus Christ. However much I wanted to make this resolution, it was not possible because I was not in control. As a teenager, my family made the decisions for me, without asking my opinion. And I had to obey whatever decisions were made if I wished to stay alive.

So even if I was determined not to go to the mosque again, when friends and family asked me to go to the mosque I had no choice but go. But I was not the same person that I was before, I just went there to show people that I was going, and that I was still with them, especially on big occasions like Eid. However I was not going back there to worship Allah again. I was merely walking into the mosque like I would walk into a boring history museum.

The bad thing was that my father did not work on Sundays so sometimes he would be at home during church time. On those days, I would not really get a chance to go to church or even try the trick of going to play soccer. And sometimes he would have things for me to do on a Sunday morning, and I had to obey. He is a man who enjoyed his sleep, so on many occasions I went to church and came back and he was still sleeping. Those were good days.

However, as time went on my father could see a change in me. For some reason I was not as enthusiastic about my Muslim faith as I was before, and this was evident not only to my father but to friends and relatives too. They figured something was wrong with me. Strangely though I seemed to have this sudden joy in my life that was not there before, so many people assumed that maybe I was seeing a girl. No one really cared too much because they thought that I was just going through a phase, and this phase would end soon and I would be back to normal.

They waited for some time but things were not going back to normal. I made it seem like I was seeing a girl, because it was a good cover plan. But I was not. Every time I got a chance I would go to church and worship with other believers in Christ. I felt so much like I belonged in the house of God, and it was always a great joy being able to go. I felt like I had a good cover, I let people assume I was going to see a girl or playing soccer, so I could keep going to church.

People grew more curious, though. They could actually see the change in me, and this was not a phase that was coming to an end, like many expected. So people starting asking about the cause of this change in my life, and I lied. On Sundays they asked where I was really going and I still lied. It would have been easy if only one person asked, but I had to lie to a whole lot of people, and I was starting to hate it. Because deep inside, I was filled with so much joy that I just wanted to explode and tell these people about my new relationship with the Savior of the world.

However, because of so much fear and worries, all that came out of my mouth were lies, and I really getting sick this feeling. One of the worst feelings I have ever experienced is having to hide how I really feel, or doing one thing while my heart is yelling out do something else. I struggled with this for a long time It was painful the times I missed going to church, and even more painful the time I had to go to the Mosque, or when felt I had to defend Islam against Christians in front of my Muslim friends.

Even on the big day called Eid, after we do the fasting when I had to dress up like a sheikh and pretend like I really enjoyed it, the times I was asked whether I was fasting during the holy month of Ramadan, I lied. All this somehow just made me feel terrible and sick of myself. I had no idea how long I was going to live with this lie. On occasions I felt every ashamed that Christ came to this earth from Heaven, He died a cruel death on the cross for me, but I was lying about Him. I was locking Him in the closet so that my people would not see Him.

Putting all the lies and shame aside, I was very happy every time I walked into the House of God; there was so much freedom there. The way we worshipped was way different from how we did in the mosque, it was such a relief to know that I could speak my language and God would listen. Thank goodness I did not have to memorize Arabic anymore. There was freedom in the House of God, we walked in and there was someone greeting you and welcoming you. There was singing and praising, people seemed like they were happy to be worshipping God.

People lifted up hands to pray, not facing a specific direction, some prayed silently, some loudly, some sat while praying, some knelt and some stood because God could hear all of them just fine. It was different. I did not have to wash myself a certain way for God to hear my prayers. There were even women in the church and on the praise team. The atmosphere was a lot less intense. The pastor cracked jokes and smiled every now and then, and he spoke my own language. I could go on and on about church. It was an awesome new experience, which very pointed much to the freedom we should have in worship.

I was having a great time at church, but trouble was brewing back at home, because the more I kept going, the more people saw me out there and they started talking. Even Christians were talking, I do not think to hurt me but in a way of saying, *look that Muslim boy is now attending church ... glory to God*. This started spreading around like a bush fire. My family, relatives and friends started hearing these rumors. However the good thing is no one believed the rumors, because of the trust they had in me, so for many it was just looked at as a rumor by Christians against a good Muslim boy, this was a common thing.

Some friends came and talked to me about the rumors of me going to church, but yet again I lied to them and said that people were just talking because they have nothing better to do. For this reason I easily put some Christians in trouble, because it seemed like they were trying to make up stuff not just about me but my entire biological family and Muslim family.

This should have served as a red flag for me to stop going to church, because it felt like I was about to get into some serious trouble. And I really wanted to, but there was something in me that deeply desired to follow

God, and draw closer to Him. So despite the trouble that was brewing, I still held onto God, and I still went to fellowship with believers in Christ. The rumors were true, I was going to church, and I could have stopped the rumors by not going but that I did not.

With the consistency of the rumors, because I kept going to church, some of my Muslim friends and family started to see some truth in the rumors. First of all I was behaving differently, and I was not the same Muslim boy that I was before. It was true I was away on many Sundays so it was not very hard for many of my people to start believing the rumors about me. So one by one they started coming to me to verify the rumors. Before they verified the rumors they reminded of the huge risks I was taking, then they told me not to follow Christian lies.

I was reminded that no one in my family was a Christian and that I would bring so much shame to my family and clan. This became very hard for me. Do not get me wrong. I loved my family and bringing shame to them was not something I wanted to do, but the really crazy thing is whatever Jesus did to my heart was real and I could not just trade it for anything in this world. Part of me just wanted to take a timeout from being a Christian and wear the Muslim mask back up again to make everyone happy until I was old enough to get away from home and get back with Christ. But Christ had created in me a passion to follow Him and it was my driving force.

That passion would not let me stop following God. Among my community and family, it was getting so serious that my grandmother (father's mother) called for me. My grandmother was a very influential member on all issues of our family; she is the figure that holds everything together. Whenever there was a problem in the family we usually went to talk to her for solutions to these problems. Basically grandmother told me to go look at the graves of all our ancestors. This was to remind me that none of them were Christian. Islam was in the family, and as long as I was born in this family, I had to follow Islam.

My grandfathers had done so much for the entire community I grew up in as far as Islam was concerned. My grandmother was not about to have her grandson follow the lies of infidels and undermine the legacy of our ancestors. My father was not the best Muslim and neither was my grandmother, but they wanted me to be better than they were. They longed for me to reach higher places as far as Islam was concerned. Most of their talks were not pointing out their own goodness. Instead, they were about was the high expectations my family had for me, and how much they desired for me to succeed as a Muslim. That explains why my father decided to spend a lot of money to put me in the best Muslim institute in Uganda, even though he himself never attended this school.

Also, my grandmother ran a restaurant in the town, where many Muslim men and women came to eat, and if they found out that her grandson had become an infidel, this would probably hurt her business. It would also ruin my family's name before many Muslims. Many would view it as a failure on the part of my father and grandmother to teach me the virtues of Islam, and groom me into a good Muslim young man. This would also change things so that my father would not be able to brag anymore about how I was excelling in learning Islam. Instead he would be ridiculed by many as a man who failed to turn his son into a proper Muslim.

I was warned, over and over again, different people talked to me. It seemed like words never served the purpose, so they resorted to action. I was warned, over and over again, different people talked to me. It seemed like words never served the purpose, so they resorted to action. I was beaten, cursed at, hated and all. It was very painful, and I hated every moment of it. I became very scared of and I started to hide from the people I once loved. I spent more time locked in my room or out in the jungle. I could sense how much people were disappointed in me just by him looking at them. I felt like, for a time there, people regretted knowing and supporting. The good relationships I once had were dying quickly.

For a long time I never looked my father straight in the eyes; I was scared to look at him, because I saw disappointment, anger and regret in his eyes. I wished to have back all those days he was very proud of me, all those days he bragged on me, and took me around with himself. Things had changed. I tried to do everything I possibly could do to please my father but nothing was good enough. The only thing that was required of me was to stop the craziness of being a Christian.

The very crazy thing was that while I was feeling pain from the beating and ill treatment I was getting for being a Christian, while my body was hurting and bruised, there was joy and peace on the inside that sweetened all that bitter pain on the outside. I should have gone crazy, become depressed, or given up, but God was keeping me in perfect peace, even when everything around me was not peaceful. I would get a heavy beating, and I would cry, but after that I was looking forward to praising and worshipping God.

At home I cried, but whenever I walked into the house of God I praised and worshipped. I was becoming an outcast among my friends, but I went into church and I felt like I belonged. That is why I strongly feel like church should be that place where everyone can go and find comfort, where rejects like me are accepted. There are a lot of people like myself, who have no place they really belong. To their parents they are a failure. They are not as good as the kids next door. They are different from what their parents want them to be. Home should be the safest place where we can run. But for some people, at home there is pain waiting for them.

It is at home that parents tell them, "I wish you were never born," and it is at home that they do not feel appreciated, valued or loved. At school it is the same thing; this kid is bullied, he is isolated from other kids, and he is called ugly names. He has no friends at school because he is not cool like the other kids. Maybe he thinks differently from the other kids. Maybe he looks and acts different from the other kids. Whatever it is, the truth of the matter is this kid does not feel like he belongs at his school.

People hate what they do not understand. So when people do not understand us, many times they will not like us. As a little boy, I saw a man in our community; this man never had a lot of friends, and he was always talking to himself. From what I heard everyone say, I grew up thinking this man was mentally ill. But as I got older I was surprised to find out that this gentleman was not mentally, or otherwise, ill. The only problem was that society treated him like he was a mad man because they did not understand him. My society never accepted him.

These people are looking for a place where they can smile again. They are looking for a place where no one will point a finger at them for being different. They are looking for a place where no one will call them crazy, ugly or outcast. They are looking for a place where they actually belong, because they are treated like strangers in their own homes, communities and schools. These people are looking for the House of God! I say this because, after I decided to follow Christ, I became one of these people.

When I got to the House of God, I understood why David, in *Psalm 122:1 I was glad when they said to me, "Let us go to the house of the Lord!"* Because the House of God is where I belong. *"My house shall be called a house of prayer for all peoples" (Isaiah 56:7).* Because I can go as I am to the House of God and He will not turn me away. In the House of God I am a beloved child, and no longer an outcast. In the House of God I should run into Love, the love of Christ. So like David, I was excited just thinking about going to the House of God.

However, for those who society does not understand or accept, it is a slap in the face when they walk into a church and see no difference between it and their homes or communities. How terrible it is when the same horrible things they endure all week become the same things they experience even in the house of God. I have felt this. Just like the Muslims rejected me, I have been to some churches that have rejected me. I have been to churches that have talked ill about me, gossiped and called me names. The only difference between them and the Muslims is that the church does a better job pretending to love.

It was a good thing that, at the first stages in my Christian walk, I was a part of a good church that encouraged me and accepted me. So even when the pressure was so heavy back at home, and people hated me in my society, I was able to focus on the people that loved me in church. This also helped me focus on God who loved me more than anything. It was not about the many that hated me, but the few that loved me, and I was going to only stick with those that loved me. I kept believing in God. I was beaten, but whips didn't seem to do the job, so one time I was beaten with a metal pipe, and that was by far the worst beating I ever received.

Maybe he thought that it would finally break me, but my passion to follow God was bigger than any beating I could get, bigger than any hatred, threats and cruelty that I got. I trusted in God to see me through this. King David wrote: *(Psalms 46)*

1. *God is our refuge and strength, a very present[b] help in trouble.*
2. *Therefore we will not fear though the earth gives way, though the mountains be moved into the heart of the sea,*
3. *though its waters roar and foam, though the mountains tremble at its swelling. Selah*
4. *There is a river whose streams make glad the city of God, the holy habitation of the Most High.*
5. *God is in the midst of her; she shall not be moved; God will help her when morning dawns.*
6. *The nations rage, the kingdoms totter; he utters his voice, the earth melts.*
7. *The Lord of hosts is with us; the God of Jacob is our fortress. Selah*
8. *Come, behold the works of the Lord, how he has brought desolations on the earth.*
9. *He makes wars cease to the end of the earth; he breaks the bow and shatters the spear; he burns the chariots with fire.*
10. *"Be still, and know that I am God. I will be exalted among the nations, I will be exalted in the earth!"*
11. *The Lord of hosts is with us; the God of Jacob is our fortress.*

The Lord Almighty was with me. Even when I was going through all the persecution, He was there with me. I did not take the beating alone; Jesus Christ took the beating with me. I was not in this fight by myself, but He was with me this whole time. He said He would not leave me or forsake me. He was the first one to give me that assurance, so I was going to stick with Him too.

It became very clear to very many that I was now an infidel and the insults had not changed me back to Islam. The threats, the friends that deserted me, the hatred, and the many times my father caned me—none of this changed me back to being a Muslim. But I trusted God who was with me that whole time.

"I've had some troubled times in this life ..." Kirk Devine said. "I've had some times where it seemed like I wasn't going to make it ... Sometimes when I didn't know whether I was coming or going ... Sometimes when I didn't know which way was up ...! But I'm glad that I had a refuge ... I'm glad that I had a place of shelter." In any sort of troubles, believers in Christ, we have a place to run. I had a place to run—God!

My family was also facing the pressure, the shame, and the insults. Many people were talking badly about my family because of me. It would have been better for me to commit some big crime than to become an infidel. That was the worst I could ever do. The criminals would have a better place in society than me. And my only crime was that I gave my life to Christ.

By now my family had tried just about everything, but never seemed to work. So one night a meeting was called at my grandmother's place, and I was given an opportunity to denounce Christ. I never did. That night I was reminded again that my father was not a Christian, and there were no Christians in my family or clan. I was told to go find another father and another family because, as an infidel, I did not belong in this family anymore. That night I was kicked out.

My auntie told me that, even if she died, I should not even go to bury her—this statement in my culture means we never ever want anything to do with you. Usually when people die, all the grudges are put to the side and there is always some kind of reunion. But that was also cancelled out when she told me never come to bury me. So just like my mother, I was kicked out. This meant that I had to find my own food, school fees, shelter and clothes. I could have gone to live with my mother, but my guilt would not let me. I was in tears as I hopelessly walked away that night.

CHAPTER 9

WHERE IS GOD?

Homeless, fatherless, rejected, and out of school, I started a new chapter in my life. In this chapter I had to depend on God and God alone because I was helpless. I had no idea what I was going to do or where I was going, but I knew and felt that God was in full control of my life. So even when things were falling apart, my life was still intact because my God was in control.

I knew God was in control but, I also found myself asking where God was. The struggles were weighing heavily on me, and the rejection made me wonder if He was still with me. Somehow I could feel His presence, but I also thought that if He was really here, then all these things would not have happened to me. Many have asked the same question like me; where is God? In the middle of all the illnesses, hunger, poverty, and deaths of our loved ones, where is God?

Where was God when earthquakes hit Japan and Haiti? Where was God when thousands of people were killed in Egypt and Syria? There were nights I walked the streets wishing God would just show up and say, "I am here." And God did show up. He was with me, but I was looking for Him to appear in the form of a good, pain-free life. Though my circumstances changed, God never moved. He is still on the throne, and He is still with us. So whenever we are brought low by such hardships, we always ought to look up, because God has gone nowhere. He still is on the throne of grace … which is like the driver's seat of this world. He is in control, and we should not be scared.

As a kid I thought my father was the best driver in the world; we would drive through bad roads, bad weather, and the car would be swinging side to side, but I was never scared, because my father was in the driver's seat. I trusted my father's driving skills because he had driven on these roads before and he was never in an accident.

If someone else was driving the car, I would have been terrified. I could not trust drivers other than my father. Still, sometimes I would get a little bit worried. But every time I looked at him in the driver's seat, and he was not worried, I had no more reason to worry. God is in the driver's seat. The bad weather might come, troubles might come, but we should not be scared because our driver is the best there is. David wrote *"I have been young, and now am old, yet I have not seen the righteous forsaken, or his children begging for bread." (Psalm 37:25).*

A couple of years after I went through the struggles I endured for becoming a Christian, I watched many television evangelists preach to the crowds that, if you receive Christ, He will make you healthy and prosperous. He will take away all your problems and life will be a walk in the park from that time on. I can't help but talk about this because it is FALSE. I have no idea where they get this gospel from.

This wealth and health gospel is not in the Bible I read. Furthermore, after I received Jesus Christ life was not a bed of roses. I was beaten, cursed, insulted, called names, hated, talked about, and rejected. There is nothing healthy and prosperous about that. The Apostle Paul was thrown in jail and was beheaded, John the Baptist was beheaded, and many other Apostles were killed for following Jesus. They did not get nice cars, or a private jet. If we are serving the same Jesus that they served, then we should expect the opposite of this health and prosperity gospel!

I do not mean to say that Christ cannot make us wealthy and healthy. He can. And He can take us to that place without any hardships. However, He does not guarantee us such things on this earth, but when we get to heaven. *"They shall hunger no more, neither thirst anymore; the sun shall not strike them,nor any scorching heat." (Revelation 7:16).* Christ certainly can bless us while we are still here on earth. He can prosper us and heal us, but this is not the reason He came to this world. What men needed and still need was not healing and money, but rather salvation. That is why Christ came. So yes, according to the true gospel, after we receive salvation we will go through hard times.

"I have said these things to you, that in me you may have peace. In the world you will have tribulation. But take heart; I have overcome the world." (John 16:33).

The problem with this prosperity gospel is that it reduces God to something like a vending machine. When you put coins in a vending machine you can press whatever you need on the menu and it will come out. These false preachers preach God is like a vending machine; we put our faith in him and money, cars, nice homes come out. Perfect health, a perfect marriage, a job, and a problem-free life will come out. The problem with this is that God is not a vending machine, and as long as we live in this sinful world, we will NOT have a perfectly prosperous, healthy life. When you look around, people are hurting from financial crises, healthy problems, and natural calamities. And all these things are happening to believers too.

So if we are taught that we are guaranteed a healthy, prosperous life in tranquility, then suffering can only mean failure in our own spiritual lives or failure on God's part to meet our expectations. Others look at it as a sign that shows God is powerless, He does not really care, or He does not really exist. These people do not put faith in God, but rather in what God is capable of doing. That might be the reason we have many church-goers looking for miracles instead of believers looking to get closer to Christ.

When we put our faith in God it will never be shaken. But when we put our faith in the things that God can do, we are bound to lose faith because God has greater aims than just to fulfill our expectations every day. We do not set the agenda for God to follow. We can't tell God, "Today give me a new car or a new job." God sets the agenda for us to follow; go out and make disciples of all nations. If it was up to us, the main aim would be something like living a long and perfect life. To God the main aim is for all men to come to His saving knowledge. God has better things to do than making us rich quick. So for those truly seeking Christ they do find Him. But those seeking miracles will be disappointed and out of church when they don't get what they signed up for.

The preachers of the wealth and health gospel are right about the fact that God will bless us when we accept Him into our lives. The problem is that God's blessings are not all material. His blessings are not only good health and promotions, as many of us look at it. God's blessings could be in the very things that are bad in our eyes. God's blessing could be joy that surpasses all human understanding that He gave me after I became a believer. God's blessings might be those times I was rejected, that drew me away from people and closer to God. God's blessings were the painful experiences I went through, because they taught me how to cry to God.

There is one thing I love about the prosperity gospel. It points to me paradise. It points to that place where we will hunger no more, where we shall not thirst anymore, where God shall wipe away every tear from my eyes. It points to that place where we will not get sick anymore, where we will not lack anything, where it will all be perfect. That place is the Kingdom of God. And we get to that place only through Jesus Christ. So we should not run to the miracles but run to Jesus Christ our Lord and Savior.

After learning about paradise, all my suffering and pain was bearable. I cried, but I cried with hope, because I knew that a time was coming when I would cry and suffer no more. I had hope that my current suffering could not be compared to the joy and the glory that awaited me in heaven through Jesus Christ. This hope kept me from quitting. The pain was just for a short time, but paradise is eternal.

So the life after receiving Jesus Christ was not a walk in the park, but it was worth it. It was even better than a walk in the park. It felt like a walk through the fire but the difference was that, as a believer, YHWH walked through the fire with me. Sometimes it doesn't really matter how long, or short, how hard or easy the journey might be. All that really matters is who is walking the journey with you. On this journey, whether on the mountain tops on the lowest valleys, I am still thankful because the Great I AM walked through with me.

"Be strong and courageous. Do not fear or be in dread of them, for it is the Lord your God who goes with you. He will not leave you or forsake you" (Deuteronomy 31:6).

As kids we went out to play soccer with other teams. But we had this one boy, Hussein, who was very good, and every time before we went out to play we had to make sure he was with us. The game would get hard but Hussein always did his magic, scored, and we won the game. It did not matter how hard the games were but who we had on our team. We had Hussein, the Miami Heat have LeBron James, the Chicago Bulls had Michael Jordan, but Christians have God. Christians have the best teammate ever. He has never lost a game.

It might get hard but God is on our team and He will see us through. Shadrach, Meshach and Abednego were thrown in the burning furnace when it was made seven times hotter than normal. But the fire did not burn them, because there was a fourth person in that fire. God was in that fire with Shadrach, Meshach and Abednego. He was on their team.

Daniel was tossed in the lions' den and he should have been devoured by those lions, but God was on Daniel's team. So even if it looked like Daniel had no chance and was going to lose, he was in the lion's Den with God. God didn't let the lions harm him.

Because God walks with us, because He is on our team, we might be hard pressed on every side but we will not be crushed; we might be perplexed, but not in despair; persecuted, but on abandoned; struck down, but not destroyed. When we decide to walk with God, God walks with us. When we get on God's team we join the team of winners and conquerors so we can walk through the fire without wavering.

CHAPTER 10

DOES GOD CARE?

So if God was somewhere, my next question was, did He care? In high school I had a person I called my friend. He was so close to me that people thought we were related. However, I had a problem one day, and that was when I learnt that, though he was close to me, he did not care about me. I honestly had the same doubts about God. I could feel that God was with me, but I wanted to know whether He cared about me. Like the disciples on a boat being tossed back and forth by storms, I wanted to ask Jesus almost the same way they did—don't you care if we perish? I simply wanted to know whether God cared!

A big part of me felt like if God cared, He would have protected me from the hatred of my father. Or maybe He would have given me a nice house to stay in, and He would have saved me from the hatred of all the Muslims. I felt like rich parents give their kids whatever they ask for, because they cared. My Father in Heaven is richer, stronger and nothing is impossible with Him. I figured He would just give me whatever I wanted—I wanted food, a house and school fees right away, but I didn't get it. So I wondered whether God cared.

Does God care? Is a question that I have heard a lot of people ask. In the Bible people asked the same question. The disciples on the boat asked the same question, "Jesus master don't you care that we drown?" Mary and Martha probably asked the same question: "Jesus your beloved friend Lazarus is dying, and we sent for you and thought you would be here immediately but you did not come, don't you care?" Did God care about Paul who was beheaded, or Elijah who was on the run for his life? Does God care?

Paul the Apostle wrote, *"To the present hour we hunger and thirst, we are poorly dressed and buffeted and homeless, 12 and we labor, working with our own hands. When reviled, we bless; when persecuted, we endure; 13 when slandered, we entreat. We have become, and are still, like the scum of the world, the refuse of all things" (I Corinthians 4:11-13).* Does God care?

Very quickly I learnt that God cared, that He cared even before I decided to follow Him. Sometimes I didn't feel like He cared because His ways were not my ways, and when I didn't understand His ways I thought that He did not care. Because if He really did care, I thought, there is no way He would have let me go through a hard time, when He has the power to give me a smooth life. The children of President Obama will not be found on the streets begging for food. Yet many of God's children go hungry and live without shelter. But I still know that God cares.

This is how I found out that God cared for me, despite the trials that I went through; even if He did not provide for me everything that I wanted, He provided all that I needed when I needed it. Somehow I never went for a whole day without a meal to sustain me. I never went begging for food but sometime someone would buy me a meal. God gave me good health, protecting me from Malaria and all other diseases. It would have been a totally different story if I had gotten sick without support.

One day I was roaming the streets, very hungry, and I ran into Pastor Godfrey Wanamitsa. I stopped to say hi to him and never told him I was hungry. But he bought me a plate of chicken and fries, at a nice restaurant, Oozies, in Jinja. I had been walking around that day wishing I had something to eat, and just like that I had a really nice meal. Pastor Godfrey was my pastor and the Ugandan partner with Rick Via World Reach Ministries.

When I read the entire Bible from the Genesis to Revelation it is all screaming out how much God cares about you and me. So it seems like an insult to God when we ask whether He cares. He cared so much that He gave us His only beloved Son to die on the cross for our sins. He cares so much that He still makes it to rain on the just and the unjust. He is still providing us with the very air we breathe. He is making warm blood run through our veins. So sounds a little bit strange when we ask whether He cares.

Therefore, when we ask the question—don't you care God?—it is only fair to reverse the question for all the other days we are not in trouble, and ask God why He cares when everything is fine! We take for granted the thirty days God has given us good health, and we whine about the few minutes we are having a headache. We take for granted the ten years we have had a job, and complain for the one week we have gone without a job. I learnt that God cared about me, even while I was still a Muslim. If He never wanted to care He could have stopped while I was still rejecting Him. Now that I was following Him, it was dumb of me to think He did not care.

He let me go through those struggles, not because He didn't care, but because He had a purpose in all the tribulations I was experiencing. The only difference was that sometimes my purpose did not line up with God's. That might be the reason I and many other people think God does not care. I just wanted to be a happy Christian and just get along with everyone, even Muslims. But God had higher purposes than just making me happy and giving me a smooth life.

I did not have a smooth life, and I still don't but I know that God cares. It was almost shameful for me when I shared the gospel and told people God cared about them. But when they looked at me, I had no home. I was not sure if I was going to eat the next meal or not, and I just did not have it all. Someone asked me does God care about you? I guess they were judging from my condition and what I owned, because to them poverty and pain did not reflect God's care.

Better yet, when Jesus was hanging on the cross, people told Him, "If you are the Son of God get off that cross." Jesus raised people from the dead, but He could not get off the cross? I mean if He was the Son of God, His

Father did not show care for Him when He let Him hang on the cross. Maybe the question in some people's minds was, if God does not care about His only Son enough to get Him off the cross how can He care about us? How could Paul preach that God cares when he spent so much time in prison?

No, God did not let Paul suffer persecuted in prison because He did not care. He did not let His only beloved Son go through all the shame and the horrible death on the cross, because God does not care. Furthermore, God let me go through my struggles not because of a lack of care, but because there was a purpose that tribulation serves, in the Kingdom of God. I learnt to look for God's purpose in every tribulation that comes my way.

God desires that all men will be saved, and often times God uses our sufferings for the purpose of drawing and saving men. Paul wrote, "*If we are afflicted, it is for your comfort and salvation" (2 Corinthians 1:6).* I wondered how men could be saved through our sufferings. If you look at the life of the prophets in the Old Testament, Jesus in the New Testament, the disciples and Paul, you will note that they all suffered publicly. Jesus was tried in public, beaten in public and hung on the cross in public. Paul was flogged in public, Job publically suffered, and Daniel suffered publically. However, on account of these public sufferings many gave their lives to God.

It is a great testimony about our God, when we are suffering, when we are persecuted and going through all sorts of trouble, if keep trusting, believing and holding on firm to our faith in God. To me one of the greatest testimony in the entire Old Testament is when Job said, " *For I know that my Redeemer lives, and at the last he will stand upon the earth" (Job 19:25).* Even when Job had lost everything, even when he was going through all sorts of troubles, Job could still testify that "My redeemer lives." This is the faith that I am talking about that will cause people to ask Job, "Who is this redeemer you believe in?"

I know we love to testify about how much God has blessed us with a new job, cars, money, marriage children and all those good things, but many times people do not see God in all these good things. They often give praise to us for working hard, for being lucky or getting a good education. When Jesus rose from the dead, it was a huge testimony, but many people said, "His disciples stole the body from the grave." This was the greatest miracle ever and many people still did not believe.

However, when Jesus was dying on the cross in public and going through excruciating pain, even at that very trying and painful moment Jesus still trusted and believed in His Father. That is why, even at this time, He could still say, "Forgive them for they know not what they are doing." And it was during this time that a dedicated Roman soldier, a cold hearted and evil man, had a change of heart as he watched Christ suffer and die on the cross. This centurion came to recognize that Christ was truly the Son of God. Maybe many more found salvation as they witnessed Christ dying on the cross.

One of the times Paul was in prison, he still believed and praised God, and moments later we read that the jailer and his whole household received salvation that day. Paul could have spent time trying to call his lawyer and cursing at people for putting him in jail even though he was innocent. However, even in a horrible place like a prison, where Paul did not deserve to be, he still lifted up the name of God in praise and worship. The end result was that the jailer and his entire household received salvation that very day.

King Nebuchadnezzar came to recognize that YHWH was the only true God, and this spread throughout the entire kingdom. But this came only after the persecution of the three Hebrew boys, Shadrach, Meshach, and Abednego in the burning furnace.

"Nebuchadnezzar answered and said, "Blessed be the God of Shadrach, Meshach, and Abednego, who has sent his angel and delivered his servants, who trusted in him, and set aside[a] the king's command, and yielded up their bodies rather than serve and worship any god except their own God.
29 Therefore I make a decree: Any people, nation, or language that speaks anything against the God of Shadrach, Meshach, and Abednego shall be torn

limb from limb, and their houses laid in ruins, for there is no other god who is able to rescue in this way. " (Daniel 3:28-29).

God chooses to reveal Himself in our weakness. In times when we are persecuted and hurt, He chooses to show men His strength. God used the suffering that I went through, many people knew that I was a young boy, and I could not survive without my family. I could not go to school. I could turn into a street kid, or worse, I could even die. But as I was hurting, the joy of God in my life was revealed. As I was weak, God's power was revealed. The people that saw me, wanted to know about this God that I clung to so tightly. The disciples turned the world upside down for Christ, and one of their biggest testimonies was the suffering and persecution they all went through.

God uses these tribulations to benefit us and not to harm us, but sometimes it was hard for me to look at my struggles this way. In many ways, I looked at struggles as a curse rather than a blessing. But through those bitter times, God develops sweet fruits in us, fruits which we cannot develop unless we go through the trying times. I love to eat cakes, but when that cake is just dough, it does not taste as good. That cake goes through a process and part of the process is fire, in the oven. It goes into that fires as dough, but when it is all done it comes out as a cake.

We go into our trials as one thing but we come out different. "*Not only that, but we rejoice in our sufferings, knowing that suffering produces endurance,*" *(Romans 5:3).*

Charles Spurgeon said, "They who dive in the sea of affliction bring up rare pearls." There are fruits, gifts, rewards or good things that we get in our lives only through suffering. We dive into the sea of affliction, but when we come out, we come out with some rare beautiful pearls. We dive into the sea of affliction but when we come out, we come out with perseverance, character, hope, and maturity. We need these gifts as believers in Christ, and they are found in the very afflictions through which we walk.

When I look back and see what God has taken me through and the fruits it has developed in me I am thankful, and I've come to realize that it was all to help me and not to break me. Now when struggles come I naturally get scared, but I look back at how God took care of me before and how God blessed me even amidst my struggle. And now I just pray and ask God for His purpose in the struggles.

There are some lessons we learn in the valleys that we cannot learn on top of the mountain. Our character is built in the valley. The people that hated me taught me to stay on my knees. They taught me not to put my trust in people but only in God. The times I lacked food taught me to depend on God as my provider, and they taught me a heart of gratitude for the times I had food. My struggles did not break me but taught me to always look to God from whom my help comes.

Afflictions are painful but they are also sweet because they cement relationships. In my country, we say you will know who genuinely loves you when times get really tough, because they will stick with you to the very end. Some of the people I am drawn to the most, are the people who were there for me when I was going through tough times. In my weaknesses I felt loved the most, because that is when I needed love the most. Sometimes the purpose of our afflictions is just to draw us in a closer relationship with God.

I was drawn closer to God, and God came closer to me in my afflictions. He became my Father, my friend, and family. Christ comes along to meet us, when we are weak and afflicted. When I read the Bible I notice that Christ could have easily spent all His time in the temple. However He was out to meet hurt people like me, the woman who had a bleeding problem, a widow who lost her only son, ten men suffering from leprosy, a man with demon attacks, blind Bartimaeus, a woman caught in adultery, and more.

When I was walking around hopelessly on the streets of Uganda, Christ met me through different people, visions and dreams. I felt His love more deeply, and I enjoyed the sweetest fellowship with Christ amidst my afflictions. Christ met me in the fire, and the fire that should have hurt me became harmless. I felt like He came very close to me during that time, He did not save me from all the afflictions but He came down and went through the afflictions with me. The same pain I was going through, Jesus Christ felt too. This magnified my understanding of his love for me.

I have been in love with two girls my entire life. The first girl I was in love with, she saw my struggles and pain, and she went through all of it with me. Anytime I got into a fight with her, I always remembered not the good times, but how many hard times we had been in together, and that kept me going. I loved her so much because those hard times cemented our relationship. It is the same with Christ; He comes and goes through the fire with us.

Let's go back to Shadrach, Meshach, and Abednego. King Nebuchadnezzar made a golden image and told everyone that when they heard the sounds of all the instruments play, they had to stop whatever they were doing and bow to worship this golden image he had made. However when the instruments played, Shadrach, Meshach and Abednego did not bow to the image. They were servants of the Most High God and they would not bow to worship any other gods other than YHWH the God of Abraham, Isaac and Jacob *(Daniel 3).*

The consequences for not bowing to the golden image were being tossed in the burning furnace. So Shadrach, Meshach and Abednego were thrown in the fire. The people who tossed them in the fire were consumed by the fire right away because it was seven times hotter than usual.

After sometime the King Nebuchadnezzar, took a look at the furnace to see how the furnace had devoured these three disobedient boys, but to his surprise the boys were not touched by the furnace. The furnace burnt everything else but the boys. Then king Nebuchadnezzar was even more puzzled because, it was not only the three Hebrew boys that he had bound and tossed in the furnace, but there was a fourth person, who looked like the Son of God. This fourth person, in fact, was Christ. Christ came into the fire with Shadrach, Meshach and Abednego.

God did not save Paul from the prison, but He saved him while he was in the prison when the angels shook the prison and the prison door all opened up so that Paul and Silas could just walk right out *(Acts 16).*

Likewise, God did not save Daniel from being tossed into the lions' den by King Darius, but God saved Daniel inside the lion's den. God locked that lions' paws, or turned those cats into some kind of cute, fat, loving Chihuahuas that would do Daniel no harm *(Daniel 6).*

Jesus Christ did not save Lazarus from the grave, but He saved him while he was in the grave *(John 11)*. I could go on and on, but I think you catch my drift by now.

There are gifts, comforts, lessons and blessings that we get only through suffering. When we avoid going through these hard times, we not only bypass the suffering but we bypass the glory of God through these sufferings. And if we go through the hard times, but get angry with God or with other people involved in our troubles, we still miss seeing the glory of God, because we exchange self-pity and anger for God's glory.

And finally, the afflictions are not meant to hurt us or break us down. We are only hurt when we fix our eyes on the troubles and take matters into our own hands. On the other hand, if we let God do his work in us through these hardships, He shapes us and our troubles into something beautiful for the Glory and Honor of His Holy name.

CHAPTER 11

A NEW DAY

"*Weeping may tarry for a night but joy comes in the morning" (Psalm 30:5).*

At night I was rejected, I wept, I was I hurt, had no school fees and I lacked. But like David, I was comforted by God's promises that my struggles were but for a short time. Indeed that night was over, and joy replaced my tears. I was back in school, assured of a meal every day and had support for my basic needs.

It does not end with the suffering and afflictions that we go through. The Bible says, *"And after you have suffered a little while, the God of all grace, who has called you to his eternal glory in Christ, will himself restore, confirm, strengthen, and establish you." (1 Peter 5:10).* The struggles and afflictions are going to hurt but only for a little while, because the morning is coming. Dying on the cross and being buried in the grave on Friday hurt for just a little while, because early Sunday morning, He rose from the grave with all power on earth and in heaven in His hands. It hurts only for a little while!

Word traveled to the Rick Via World Reach Ministry team about my situation, and soon enough they started sending me financial help. I was put back into school, and my tuition was fully paid. I now had money to afford a meal every day and a place to stay. During this time Pastor Godfrey played a major role in my life. He didn't have me stay at his house but every now and then he invited me over. He became the father figure in my life during this time. I called his wife "Mommy," and I enjoyed playing with his kids. As a matter of fact one of his son's was named Emma, same as me. I enjoyed these time because I felt like I was a part of a family again, and these were joyful moments.

Things were starting to fall in place, and I just had that big sigh of relief thinking that it is all over now; the pain is gone and the suffering is finished. In a negative way this affected my prayer life, I felt less urge to pray as constantly as I used to amidst my afflictions. I had the mindset that, it has been a hard bumpy ride, and now I could sit back, relax and enjoy the smooth ride. I stopped reading the word as much as I used to. Like some people say, I took my foot off the gas pedal.

Maybe it was just me, or maybe it is a natural reaction for man to take a break every now and then. In basketball games, timeouts are just a part of the game. At work, vacations are needed. In school, we take breaks. So I felt like taking a timeout too, and enjoying my break from all the struggles I had been going through. As I prayed less and read my Bible less, pride crept in and slowly I became a different person.

One thing my pride wanted was to show Muslim friends who deserted me, and those waiting for me to crumble in the hard times, that now I had money. My tuition was fully paid for, I was assured of good food every day, and I even had money to buy some new clothes. I remember going to an expensive restaurant not because I wanted to eat there, but just to show that I was doing better than everyone thought.

A friend told me that our spiritual lives are mainly affect by two things, success and disaster (afflictions and sufferings). These two determine whether you will still trust and follow God diligently. With disaster some people run away from God. With success some people take a break from serving God to enjoying their success. I was enjoying coming out of my struggles successfully, but success on the outside was hurting my spiritual growth.

I have seen and heard of people who used to diligently seek God, back when they were living on a budget. But since financial success came in, they have no time for God because they have to be out enjoying their riches, maybe on vacation somewhere playing golf. I have heard about preachers who started out preaching the Word of God faithfully, but since they became successful, now it is all about getting more money and being more successful rather than leading the flocks of God.

Success is a good thing, but if we get our eyes off of Him who gives us success, we are bound to fall into the traps of the enemy. When the tough times phased out, and I was generally having a good time I took a timeout and the devil had a feast on me. The Bible says, *"Be sober-minded; be watchful. Your adversary the devil prowls around like a roaring lion, seeking someone to devour." (1 Peter 5:8).* Those people who have taken a timeout are a great feast for the devil.

In the jungles of Africa the zebras and gazelles have to be watchful all the time when they are in a lion's territory, they can't relax and take a nap there or they will be eaten. As believer I live in the devil's territory (the world), and I just can't afford to take a timeout or slow down because the devil never takes a timeout. He is on a mission to steal, kill, and destroy. The race is not over when it gets easier, the race is over only when we get to the finish line. Our finish line has been set in heaven, so until we get to heaven we cannot take a timeout. We have to keep running.

Remember, when David should have been at battle with the rest of the Israelite army, he took a timeout to stay home and relax. However, this is when King David, a man after God's heart, fell into the traps of the enemy to lust and commit adultery with Bathsheba, the wife of Uriah. We can take a time out in a basketball game, but on the spiritual journey we cannot.

The Via's sent me financial support from America through Pastor Godfrey Wanamista. However, Pastor Godfrey was about to visit America. So before he left, he decided to give me all the money I would need for the next semester, food and other needs. It was about one hundred dollars. I would like to pause right here, and confess that up to that point, I had never seen that kind of money before. I was very scared of even having that money on me, I feared someone would rob me or kill me. I felt like the richest man in the world. I decided to have my friend Dan pick up the money for me because I just did not want to take the risk of walking around with that much money.

Dan was older than I was and he had a dream of becoming a gospel artist and going all over ministering through music. I joined him but music was not really my calling. Besides, I could not sing to save my life. Dan picked the money up, and somehow he thought it would be great to buy new clothes for us to look good when we went out to sing.

This money was meant to take care of me and to pay for my tuition for the next semester, not to buy new cool clothes. Using this money on anything else was the wrong thing to do, but I had taken a time out, and the devil had taken over. So instead of saying no we should not buy clothes, I just agreed with Dan. I said that would be a great idea, take the money and do what you have to do.

He took it and bought clothes, and I saw very little of the money. What I did see of it, I used to buy food and even give away to some people; I thought I was Donald Trump. For some reason I thought that hundred dollars would last forever, but I was in for a big surprise. That money did not even last a month. Though I needed it to last longer, I found out the hard way that hundred dollars disappear rather quickly. We bought the good-looking clothes to look good on stage, and it felt good but that was not what the money was meant for. I was not a good steward.

Vacation was almost over, and it was about time to go back to school for the new semester, but I did not have money to pay for tuition food and housing. So I was waiting for Pastor Godfrey to come back from America and give me money.

Pastor Godfrey came back from America, and when I asked him for tuition for the upcoming school term he reminded about the hundred dollars. Pastor Godfrey told me, "I left you money to take care of all this before I went to America. Why are you asking for more money?" And that is when it hit me that I had sinned, the whole time I had not looked back to think what I had done with the money was wrong, until this time. Because I had taken a time out, the devil was making wrong seem right to me until Pastor Godfrey reminded me.

I had no idea how or what to tell Pastor Godfrey, words never came out of my mouth. All I was asking myself was how in the world I had sinned without even noticing it. I started thinking how awful I was, on the streets when I had nothing and all I wished for was at least one dollar to live on, but God gave me more than one dollar—I had one hundred dollars and misused all of it. When I looked back, I realized that I started falling into sin the minute I decided to take my foot off the pedal.

Pastor Godfrey had no money to give me, so I walked away very sad and very ashamed. I knew that I was destined for life back on the streets searching for food to eat. To make it worse, at this point I had made some enemies, all those Muslims I showed off too, telling them I was doing great even without their help. It rubbed some the wrong way who had expected to see me crumble and return to Islam. So I was threatened and had heated confrontations out on the streets. People conspired to put me in prison saying I had stolen money from someone.

I remembered Pastor Godfrey telling me that Jared Via literally washed people's toilets to raise support for me. I do not know about America but in Uganda washing toilets is one of the worst jobs anyone could have. This did not make me feel better at all, because I thought, Jared is doing the lowest job, to give me a good life and I just blew it. I felt bad, awful and full of sin. I not only let Jared and the Rick Via team down when I took a timeout. I let God down. God gave me the best He could give, and Christ lived the lowest life and died a shameful death so that I can live, but I was not living like I was supposed to live.

It was very selfish of me to think I needed a timeout. Have you ever stopped to think where we would be if God took a timeout? What would happen to us if He who watches over Israel actually slumbered? It was bad enough that I had sinned, however now guilt was waging another battle on me. Guilt made me feel like I had messed up and lost the love of my supporters. It had been the history in my life; I had short spells when I felt love, but the people who loved me would end up leaving soon. I thought these loving friends too were about to leave me. However, this time around, it was totally my fault. Guilt told me that I did not deserve their love anymore.

So, out of guilt, I was very scared to even contact my supporters. I cut off contact with them, and I went back to my old life of trying to find something to eat on my own. And as the school semester was drawing close, I had lost hope of joining school again. I thought that my supporters were very mad and disappointed in me, that they would not even talk to me again. In fact, some Ugandans at Arise Africa International who knew about it were also very disappointed in me, though they gave me no money at all. The people who actually gave the money must have been much more disappointed.

Going to church became very hard. As a matter of fact, shortly after that I quit going to the church because I was constantly reminded of the wrong I had done. The church I was attending was also supported by the Rick Via World Reach Ministries. Sometimes people were not talking about me, but anytime I saw a group of people talking and laughing, all they had to do was take one glance at me and I thought they were talking about me. Guilt was taking its toll on me.

The devil used temptation to draw me into sin, but used guilt to keep me in bondage to sin. The same devil that tempted me into being a bad steward one minute, he told me how awful, evil, messed up, and worthless I was. It was the same devil telling me I was not good anymore. This is why I condemned myself and stopped contacting my supporters. Satan used guilt to rob me of my confidence and faith in Jesus Christ. And that is when I stopped going to church, and I isolated myself because I felt like I was evil and didn't belong with the holy people in church.

Guilt will make us run even when no one is chasing us. Jacob was running from Esau, but Esau was not really pursuing Jacob. Adam and Eve ran and hid from God, but He was not really chasing them. I was running from my supporters and Pastor Godfrey but they were not chasing me. Guilt made it seem like the whole Christian world was against me for what I had done.

Jesus said, "The thief comes only to steal, kill and destroy" (John 10:10), and one of the enemy's weapons is guilt. Guilt will make us run away from the people or places we should be running to for help. And instead of running to help, we run to destruction. We run right into the devil's traps, so we get destroyed and give victory to the devil. If Judas Iscariot realized that he had sinned against Christ, and had run to Christ for help, he would have been better off. However, the devil used guilt to make Judas run right into the enemy's trap, and guess what happened? That day the enemy stole, killed and destroyed Judas' life.

Many of us do struggle with guilt because of the wrong things we did in the past. We struggle to believe that God can forgive us, we cannot forget our sins, and there is a lot that continually reminds us of the evils we committed in the past. Sometimes, worse than that, we condemn ourselves and find it very hard to forgive ourselves. There are things in our past we wish we had never done, we wish we were smarter-- guilt eats us away slowly.

However, there are two kinds of guilt. The **positive** guilt leads us to repentance, and the negative one is used by Satan to steal and destroy our lives. "*For* godly grief *produces a repentance that leads to salvation without regret, whereas* worldly grief *produces death." (2 Corinthians 7:10).* By "grief," I believe this scripture is relating to guilt. Positive guilt will cause us to realize that we have sinned against a holy God, and cause us to turn away from our sins and turn to God for our salvation, forgiveness and freedom from our sins. After King David committed his sin with Bathsheba, Prophet Nathan had a conversation with him about him. By the end of the conversation, King David came to understand just how bad he had sinned against God and Uriah.

This is when guilt set in, but it was not the same guilt that Judas felt. This guilt was Godly. This guilt did not lead King David to kill himself but drove him to repent of his sins *(Psalms 51).* This is good guilt and everyone should have this kind of guilt, because in the end this guilt frees us from sin. But the negative guilt is only from Satan and it is meant to keep in bondage and kill us.

As I went out to share the gospel with different people the most common thing I heard people say was, "You have no idea what I have done. I messed up big time, and God would not want to take me." It is that satanic guilt that is keeping people in bondage. It makes them think what they have done is too bad, that they do not deserve forgiveness. God does not look at how big our sins are, but He is looking to see if we can accept His Son's work on the cross and take the gift of salvation.

No one is good enough, not even the Christians. The only thing that qualifies us is that we are in Christ. So guilt tells us how bad we are and rightly so, but grace says we can be righteous if we get in Christ. So we make a decision to entertain our guilt and die in our sins, or realize that we are guilty and in need of a savior. When people say they have done some very sinful thing in their lives, I let them know that Christ paid a hefty price for those very sinful things. And the fact that we realize how far we have fallen should push us even more to know Christ.

Jesus Christ already died on the cross at Calvary for all our sins, big or small. When we receive Christ in our lives the Bible says that we are in Christ. If I had a book and I folded up a piece of paper, put it in the book, and close the book, what will be seen is not that paper inside the book, but the book that the folded paper is in. As believers in Christ, we are that folded paper in the book, God does not see our sinful selves, but He sees His sinless Son Jesus Christ that we are in.

In my guilt the enemy condemned me, he let me know how much of a loser I was, how much I failed, and how big my fault was. Condemnation has one end: destruction. Condemnation does not seek to find a solution, but looks to magnify the problem, and to tear you down. But in Christ, God does not condemn us, for there is no condemnation for those who are in Christ. Jesus never came to the world to condemn it *(John 12:47)*, but to save the world.

I learnt some practical lessons on how to deal with guilt from *Philippians 3:13-14. "Brothers, I do not consider that I have made it my own. But one thing I do: forgetting what lies behind and straining forward to what lies ahead, 14 I press on toward the goal for the prize of the upward call of God in Christ Jesus."*

The first point I learnt is that I needed to forget the sins in the past; I think the reason Paul talks about forgetting his past here is because it was full of bad things, mistakes and regrets. These things would hinder his outlook onto a bright future in Jesus Christ. Paul persecuted the church, and many Christians died because of Paul. He calls himself the chief sinner because of all the awful things he did.

However, Paul had turned the page, and was willing to move forward and not live in the past, because those who are in Christ are new creatures. I know it is hard for many people to let go of the past. People easily still hold onto things that happened 20 years ago. The truth is what I did yesterday does not determine who I am going to be tomorrow. If he had held onto the past, Paul would not have been the great apostle we know. We have to understand that God forgives us and washes away our sins regardless of what we did wrong, so we have to let go of our past guilt and gain more of Christ. Forgetting the sins of the past begins with turning away from those sins and turning to God. Once we have done that, we just need to look forward, and keep moving till we reach the finish line.

Secondly, I learnt the need to reach for the High Calling of God in the Present; I could not change the wrongs I did in the past, but I had an opportunity to do right in the present. Paul was a very bad man in the past. He persecuted Christians but now he had an opportunity to live for God. We all have an opportunity, today you and I can live for God. Today we can have a fresh start, and the wrongs we did yesterday will not even matter. Today we can be fishers of men. Today we can get up back on our feet and start running the race God has set for us, but we must be determined to let go of the past and live in the present.

Finally, I learnt the need to press towards the future; not living in the past, living in today, and now I had to live with my eyes set on the future. As a believer in Christ my future is bright, because at the end of it all, I will win. Living for Christ today and looking forward to winning the prize He has for us is the most exciting part of it all, and one reason we should not live in past guilt.

When we let negative guilt in, we give way to condemnation, and bypass grace. I condemned myself, I thought that the best thing would be to go away from Church and write off my supporters. But grace was saying, "I do not condemn you, you should go and sin no more." One of the unique things about God is that His love for us does not depend on what we are doing right or wrong. God's love for us is unconditional, He loves us anyways. Even when I had made that mistake God was still blessing me, I could still feel God's presence. He gives us a second chance and a third chance and a fourth chance and more.

"Though we are incomplete, God loves us completely. Though we are imperfect, He loves us perfectly. Though we may feel lost and without compass, God's love encompasses us completely ... He loves every one of us, even those who are flawed, rejected, awkward, sorrowful, or broken." – Dieter F. Uchtdorf

CHAPTER 12

GRACE AND UNCONDITIONAL LOVE

Growing up I always knew that love and gifts came after I behaved well, and the many times I did not behave well, I was always punished. Basically I always got what I deserved. After I misused the money that was given to me, I knew that I deserved a punishment, condemnation and rejection. So before my supporters passed judgment to me I judged myself and left my supporters and church. But regardless of my unfaithfulness my supporters loved me, so when I ran away they chased after me, not to punish me but to embrace and love me.

In America the Rick Via World Reach Ministries was preparing a missionary, who was to come to Uganda to serve as a long time missionary. When this missionary got to Uganda I had a chance to meet him. He told me that one of the things he was asked to do by Rick Via before he got on the plane for Uganda was to find a former Muslim boy Emma (me), take care of him, bring him back to church, put him in school and disciple him. This reminded of the unconditional love God gave me that, while I was yet a sinner, He sent His Son to die on the cross for me.

Things were finalized in America, so Terry Nester and his family sold their belongings and house and moved to Uganda to be long-term missionaries. However, when they got to Uganda I really didn't know about it. Because of my guilt, I had separated myself from the church and the people that supported me. But one of my favorite ladies in this entire world, Debbie

Ireson, reached out to me by email, and told me that Terry Nester and his family were in Uganda. And she asked me to pay them a visit.

I got her email a few days later, and even when I read it, I did not go right away. I figured, if these missionaries were sent by Rick Via Ministries, they probably knew about my unfaithfulness with money. Therefore I thought that they would want nothing to do with me. Besides they were staying at Arise Africa International, and I had been away from that place for some time because people there were not happy with my bad stewardship.

A few days later, I was playing on the internet again, and I got another email from Debbie asking me whether I went to meet these missionaries. I had not gone to meet them yet, but her persistence made me want to go see them. Debbie also was well aware of what I had done, but she still loved me anyway. So one day I went to Arise Africa International where these missionaries were staying. And I thought that even if they condemned me, they would at least give me some food to eat, since I visited in good time for lunch.

I went to Arise Africa International, and sure enough there was this big white guy there who looked like a missionary. I walked up to him, and he had a big smile on his face. Somehow it felt like he knew me, maybe from pictures, I figured. He was on the Rick Via World Reach Ministries team that I served with when I first got saved. However I just could not remember him well at first because he was older and I had only hung out with younger people or Debbie Ireson.

Anyway, he sat me down and his eyes started to get watery like he was about to cry, and I was thinking to myself, *What have I done so wrong to make a big guy like this one cry?* Terry told me that he had sold everything he owned in America to come start a new life with his family as missionaries in Uganda. With tears in his eyes, Terry opened a yellow notebook, he turned to a page, and showed it to me, this page had my name on it (Ismail) and Terry told me, "Today I prayed for you."

Terry went on to say, "I have come to be a long time missionary in Uganda, but before I left one of the things I was asked to do by Rick Via was to find you and take care of you." My heart melted, I do not know exactly how to describe the emotions I was going through at that point. I was thinking to myself how in the world does God still care for me? How can my supporters still provide for me after what I did?

I do not know how the woman caught in adultery felt when Jesus told her, "Neither do I condemn you," but I can tell you that at that point I felt the same words being spoken to me, "Emma, I do not condemn you." I felt forgiven and given another chance to do better next time. I always thought God's blessings came through material stuff, or when He gives me good health, but I witnessed God's blessings through His grace and forgiveness for me. I am a very blessed man; I do not know too many people that mess up and still get love like I did.

After spending some time talking to Terry, I later met the rest of his family, his wife Debbie, his daughter Natalie, and his son Jonah. And I will just skip to the middle of the story and let you know that these four people eventually became my family. God's promise of "I will be a mother to the motherless and a father to the fatherless" came to pass in my life through the Nester family. Terry became my dad, Debbie my mom, Natalie my sister and Jonah my brother. They all became very precious to me.

I was out of school at this point, and it was already too late to get into school because most schools had stopped registering new students. But Pastor Terry prayed, and told me the next day we should go try to get into a school that was nearby. We got on bikes, the most common means of transport in my town, and went to apply to this school called Jinja Secondary School.

When we arrived at the school there were notes everywhere saying, "We are not taking in anymore students." As if we could not read English, we still went into the office and applied. My grades from my last school were good, and God was on our side, so that about 15 minutes later I was a registered student of Jinja Secondary School. And by the next week all my tuition was paid in full, and I was assured of shelter at the school hostel.

Yes, these great things were happening, and I was very happy. However, in the back of my head I still struggled with guilt, despite the kindness Terry and his family had shown me so far. I kept waiting for the point when Terry Nester would sit me down to scold and condemn me for misusing the funds I was sent. I lived in fear, every time he called to talk to me, I kept thinking, "This is it." Those first few days together were not fun, because instead of enjoying our time together, I kept waiting for the condemnation and punishment. I waited for a long time, and Terry never gave me the condemnation that I was looking for.

I am not different from a man in the Old Testament named Mephibosheth, the Son of Jonathan and the grandson of Saul. Saul and his family were enemies of David. On a couple of occasions, Saul hunted David down with the goal of killing him. Another member from Saul's family line, Ishbosheth, the nephew of Mephibosheth, also tried to kill King David, but David defeated him. To be secure, it would only make sense if David went on to kill everyone in Saul's family just to prevent any further opposition or rebellion from Saul's family.

So Mephibosheth lived in fear that sooner or later David would find him and kill him. Mephibosheth was hiding from King David because he expected condemnation, judgement and death. David maybe would have been right to judge and kill Mephibosheth, but King David gave this man grace. Instead of receiving the king's wrath and judgment, Mephibosheth received grace and adoption as a son. It was by grace that Mephibosheth's life was turned around. He was given a better house to stay in, he had better provision, and he got a new family; he was adopted as a son in David's family.

That day Mephibosheth was hiding and waiting to be attacked, but grace came knocking, and when grace comes knocking everything changes. I was hiding and keeping away because of guilt, but God showed me His grace through Terry Nester and Rick Via. Grace is giving me what I do not deserve; after my evil I did not deserve their help but they still helped me. Like David with Mephibosheth, Terry didn't show me his wrath for my mistakes, but returned grace, he put me in school, put food on the table, gave me a home and made me a part of his family.

And when I got a taste of that grace, it actually led me to break down and repent to the Nesters, I told them that I was wrong in how I had spent the money that was given to me. But I was ready to be a better steward starting from that day. They forgave me. I remember Natalie telling me it was not the end of the world. She said many teenagers make a lot of bad decisions when it comes to money.

Though many church people who knew about this issue had already passed condemnation to me, they had already decided that I had messed up and did not deserve anymore help, the Nesters did not condemn me. Yes they recognized that what I did was wrong and wanted me not to do that again, but they corrected in love and not condemnation. Because grace condemns condemnation.

What the Nesters did helped me have a glimpse of God's grace for me in general. Men disobeyed God, men turned against the God that created them. The God that provided and gave them life, they turned against and worshipped idols. Men shook their fingers in God's face, and men provoked God to anger. It's as if they were saying, "We will kill, we will steal, we will bare false witness and take your name in vain, and there is nothing you can do about it God."

If you watch movies you have probably seen a scene where the main actor who, by the way is very strong and can beat up everyone, is provoked … but he might restrain his anger for some time. But the bad guys go too far, they cross the line, they mess with his family. At this point the actor is thinking I have had enough, and he goes on a killing spree where he kills all the bad guys. Whenever I watch these movies I just can't wait for that part where the hero is fed up with all the provocations and just decides to kill all the bad boys.

Men have provoked God enough, that He would have be justified if He'd gotten very angry and wiped out all men from the face of earth. But He did not do that, instead He repaid men's cruelty with kindness. He returned men's hate with love. No one deserves this, but because of grace, God gives us what we do not deserve. So it taught me not to be scared of Terry and his family. But more importantly, it helped me learn that God's throne is not a throne of judgment but a throne of grace, so I could approach His throne without fear but with confidence.

I learnt about God's grace, but I also learnt that I should deal graciously with other people too because we are all saved by grace and grace alone. If we are going to imitate a gracious savior, I learnt that we should deal graciously with others, just like the Savior deals with us. However, we are living in a day and time where many of us prefer passing judgment and condemnation while neglecting grace.

This makes us not very different from the Scribes and Pharisees. In John 8, the Scribes and Pharisees brought unto Jesus a woman taken in adultery, they sat her in their midst and told Jesus how it happened. This woman was caught in adultery in the very act. We like to say she got caught with her hand in the cookie jar. There was no need for a lawyer, her accusers were right, there were enough witnesses. The woman did not even need to defend herself because she knew and everyone knew what she had done. Now the only thing everyone was waiting on judgment and condemnation.

This woman was dragged into the temple. I have no idea if her accusers allowed her to even get fully dressed or put some makeup on to be ready to be in public. I doubt they did, so I am assuming that she was not fully dressed. I could only imagine the shame she went through by her faults being made public in such a disgraceful way. Maybe she just wished for them to get on with it, kill her and spare her the shame.

She had had enough. She did not need another person to tell her shame on you, she did not need another person to call her names, and she didn't need another person to condemn or accuse her. All she really needed was grace. This woman stood alone, the law was against her, because it is the law that commands she should be stoned, and the crowd was against her because they were the ones about to stone her.

I mentioned before that when grace comes knocking lives are changed. That day this woman came face to face with grace when she met Christ. Christ was not there to say, "Shame on you, what were you thinking?" or even "Stone her." Christ simply said to her, "I do not condemn you woman. Go and sin no more, because my grace is sufficient." Yes, Jesus hated her sins but He loved her and forgave her. And she was only going to be saved by grace, not by condemnation.

Grace was the answer, and it should be the answer in many of the issues we deal with concerning other people's faults. All have sinned and fallen short of the Glory of God. So no one deserves to throw a stone at anyone else, because they are just as bad as whoever they are stoning. Christ did not stone me for my sins, the Nesters did not stone me for misusing funds, and God is calling me to drop the stones and pick up grace.

CHAPTER 13

BACK TO SCHOOL

In my country, education is considered the most important gift a father can give his children. I had lost that gift but the Nesters gave me back that gift, and two years later I was able to graduate from high school. During these two years I was never sent home for school fees because all my tuition was paid up front, and all my school needs were fully provided for by the Nesters and Rick Via Ministries. This was a blessing to go from having nothing to having everything I could ask for regarding school.

I was accepted in Jinja Senior Secondary School, and I began life there as a student. I stayed in the hostel, but over the weekends I visited the Nester's residence. I helped them clean the yard, I played with Jonah, and spent time learning from Pastor Terry. From him I learnt not only about the Bible but about how to be a man. Visiting the Nester's home was whole new experience for me, because I had never been in an American home before. Mama Debbie made meals that were out of this world. It was only after I ate her food that I started to desire going to America.

I thought to myself, *if this is what Americans eat all the time, then Lord, please send me to America!* Jonah and I would literally spend hours just talking about food. He showed me pictures of American food. He told me of all the great food out there that I was missing out on. From the first week I met Jonah I knew that we would be great friends because we both were gifted eaters; eating or even just talking about food made us happy.

At the lunch table I always ate super-fast. Before everyone even got going I was usually finished with my plate and ready for the next serving. Debbie and Natalie always told me to slow down, that no one was going to take my food away. They never understood that this was heaven for me and I was not going to take my time. I always joked that Christ would come back to take us to heaven anytime when we are not expecting Him, so I couldn't slow down when it came to food. If Christ came, I wanted to go on a full stomach. Visiting the Nesters and eating their food made me wish I was born in America.

The Nester's home became my favorite place to hang out. I went to school from Monday to Friday, but I could not wait for Saturday to come so I could go visit the Nesters and eat some heavenly food. I was excited to see the Nesters, but I was really more excited about the food. Their home was close to my school so sometimes, even if it was not a Saturday, I would make some excuse to go over

My appetite for Ugandan food started fading away, and at school I slowly stopped eating cafeteria food. I would tell students how good the American food was. Sometimes, when I went to bed, I saw this food in my dreams. I wanted badly to visit America. One time Terry asked me to choose one food that I would want to have if it was my birthday, and I picked meatloaf over all the Ugandan food I had grown up eating. Mama Debbie made the best meatloaf; to this point I have never had better meatloaf than hers.

One time I joked with the Nesters that, if we just feed the Ugandans some American food and then tell them this exact food will be in heaven, heaven would be packed full of Ugandans in one day. Just like that I figured out the quickest way to do evangelism—food evangelism.

Jonah and I would fill up our plates so high, and we would joke about that scripture that says, "You will have faith to move mountains." We practiced our faith on the Food Mountains that we had piled up on our plates. These mountains were moved in a couple of minutes. I was having so much fun every time I hung out with Jonah, because of our shared love for food.

I might seem to be crazy for food, but I could not help that the Nester's place was the first where I ever had that kind of food.

One Saturday, I visited from the hostel and this time the Nesters let me spend the night. Like many Ugandan boys I always had body odor, because I did not use deodorant. I had no idea I stunk. I just figured I was alright since no one ever told me, "You stink." However, Jonah could not stand my body odor, especially after we ran around playing, so he told me to take a shower before we did anything else.

I got into the bathroom, and all I saw was a bunch of bottles but no soap. In Uganda, I had only showered with bar soap. I turned the water on, and hot water came out. I had never seen that before, either. I wanted to touch the bottles, but I didn't know which bottle did what. Or the side effects it would have on black skin. So I let water run over me and I was done. Everything was very new in the bathroom; I felt like I needed lessons on how to shower in an American bathroom.

Jonah had prepared clean clothes for me, but when I got out of the bathroom I still smelled the same as before I got into the shower. Jonah sat me down and taught me how to shower. We went back to the bathroom, and he showed me the stuff I needed to use. In total I used stuff from three bottles: body wash, shampoo and conditioner. Before, I only used a bar of soap.

The stuff from the bottles smelled really good, and when I walked out of the bathroom this time, I was a different person. I smelled so good, I liked myself, and this time Jonah approved. He gave me something to put under my armpits which made me smell even better. That night was the first time in my life, thanks to Jonah, that I used deodorant. After using it, and smelling good, I became sensitive to the odor of Ugandans boys. In class I smelled good and even the girls liked it. I started telling my friends, "Dude you stink," though they never understood why I thought that.

After showering, Jonah gave me clean clothes, and we went downstairs to have dinner and watch a movie all together. After the movie, we had to sleep early so we could get up early for church the next day. I slept in

Jonah's room, but Jonah and I fell asleep later because we were up talking. So when everyone got up early that morning for breakfast, we were still in bed. But this morning is one of my favorite memories with the Nesters.

Terry came in to wake us up for breakfast; remember I told you Terry was a big guy. Jonah and I had slept on the same bed. Terry jumped in between us that morning. He tickled Jonah till he woke up, and then I felt his big fingers tickling me too moments later, and then he said, "Rise and shine!" This felt so good, and this was the first time ever that I woke up with a smile on my face. That morning I felt the physical touch of a parent, and for the first time ever, it was not punishment.

It's been years but I have never told Terry about this. I feared he would think that it was just something small, that maybe he never even thought much about it before he did it. However small it might seem to him, to me it was big. Somehow I felt loved. I do not remember anytime that my parents ever woke me up like that. This goes to remind us that the things we do, however small they might be, if we do them in love, they can go a long way. Small loving things can have huge impacts on people's lives. This is still one of my favorite memories.

As time went by, I would visit the Nesters over the weekends, but the semester was coming to an end. During vacation I would get to spend every day with them. Indeed, vacation came and I spent the days at the Nester's house then spent nights at my friend Jeb's house. I wanted to just live with the Nesters, but I believe that, for many different reasons I did not know, they were not quite ready to have me move in yet.

However, after sometime they let me move it with them, and I slept in Jonah's room. I was extremely overjoyed that they let me move in, but I found even more joy in knowing that I was not moving in as a visitor but as a son in the house. There was a guest room in the house and the children's rooms. I was put in the children's room with Jonah. The guest room was empty, and maybe they could have sent me there, but I was not treated as a guest in the house.

I was in the right place because I loved spending time with Jonah. We often stayed up late talking, and on one of those nights we started a new tradition at home that we called "the midnight snack." This was one of our favorite times because it was just Jonah and me and the food we loved to eat. We would wait till everyone went to sleep, then we snuck to the kitchen to get our midnight snacks and have our midnight fellowship. These moments brought us very close to each other.

Midnight snack was a fun thing just for me and my brother Johan. No one else was invited to join, not even Natalie. Every time she joined it was never that fun (... she is not going to like me for this). She said uncool things like, "Clean the kitchen after the snack," or "It is getting too late—go to sleep." So we excluded her. Terry and Debbie could not join because they probably would stop our mid-night fellowship altogether. They were a little bit older and were not as cool as Jonah and I.

Somehow word got around that Jonah and I were meeting up for this midnight snack fellowship. So some people at home tried to join or stop our fellowship. Therefore we came up with a plan to exclude others from our brotherly bonding project, so we went to sleep when everyone went to sleep. Correction: we pretended to go to sleep when the others went to sleep. Once we were sure everyone was in bed, then it was time to get on with our midnight snack.

At the Nesters I was introduced to cereal, and I fell in love with it, especially the chocolate kind. So during midnight snack time, I always knew exactly what I was going to eat. It has been over seven years now, and I still love cereal. I think it is one of the best things ever invented.

It was always fun because we had to sneak downstairs (it was a two story house and the kitchen was downstairs). The doors made noise, the stairs squeaked, and lights were off, so we made noise too. Sneaking down was fun, because we both just wanted to break out in laughter but we couldn't because we would wake everyone up. Regardless we always found a way to get to the food. I do not know if Terry and Debbie heard us and just let the boys have some fun or if we were just really good at sneaking. Some of these times the doors sounded louder than usual, and the stairs squeaked even louder.

Mama Debbie would get into the kitchen in the morning and see two used cereal bowls lying on the counter. Some chocolate cereal balls were lying on the kitchen floor, and the milk bottle was somehow half empty or empty. I guess she did the math and figured two people were sneaking down to eat. It could not have been Terry and her because they were sleeping. It could not have been Natalie because she was alone. There were only two people who enjoyed eating and had larger appetites than everyone else in the family. And there was especially one boy who loved cereal that much.

In a funny way Mom asked who it was while we were sitting around the dinner table. For some strange reason everyone looked at me and Jonah, but we looked up to the ceiling. Mama said that, if it was her sneaking down to eat, she would not leave a mess but would leave the kitchen the way it was. If you asked me, I would tell you that Mom knew exactly who these two people were, but she loved them and just let them have some boy time. As a matter of fact, one time while we were having our midnight snack, a bigger older boy joined us. You can guess who. We ate together, but that night our fellowship was very short and not as fun. That explains why it had to be only me and Jonah.

The only bad thing about midnight snack was getting up in the morning when everybody else got up, because we had to have breakfast and morning devotions together as a family. I would walk down the stairs with one eye half way open, and I remember Mom would say something like, "Looks like someone was up eating cereal last night." The sweet smell of breakfast always helped me completely wake up, because food just had that effect on me. And every morning, Mom would say sweet things like, "Good morning honey," "Sweetie," "Sunshine," and such sweet names that I had never been called before. So getting out of bed was hard, but it worth it because of all the love that was waiting for me first thing in the morning.

CHAPTER 14

TOGETHERNESS

Ricardo Montalban said, "True love doesn't happen right away; it's an ever-growing process. It develops after you've gone through many ups and downs, when you've suffered together, cried together, laughed together." In other words true love and togetherness are inseparable. I felt truly loved by the Nesters, and I truly loved back. When I hurt they hurt, when I laughed they laughed, and when I was sad they were sad. At the Nesters it was not Emmanuel anymore. It was us, we, The Nesters.

Every morning we had breakfast together as a family. Even when Jonah and I were up late having midnight snack, we had to be at the breakfast table with everyone in the morning. Right after breakfast we shared devotions and sometimes each person got a chance to say something during devotions. I was new in the family and not as spiritually mature as everyone else, but I was also given a chance to say something, because we were doing it all together. And at the end of devotions we held hands and prayed for each other.

Sometimes during lunch, I got upset because food was ready, and I just wanted to dig in, but we had to wait for the last member of the family to join before we started eating. We have a saying in my mother tongue that says, "The tree cannot fall on someone who is not there." We used this saying a lot when it came to food, if someone was not there we just went on to eat. For a long time I didn't like the waiting and eating together thing, until it was me who was being waited on. They waited for me to get home and eat with them.

Togetherness, like I experienced at the Nesters, was a brand new thing to me, but I was really starting to enjoy it. The life I was used to was different; my dad did his own thing, my mother took care of our home, and the kids did their own thing. There was never a time my family just went out to do something together. There are time everyone at the Nester family was shooting basketball, even Mom and Natalie. Not because they were really good at it but because they loved to do things together as a whole family.

Some Saturday afternoons, the family went out to swim. However, I am very scared of being in water. I always joked around that, if I had to swim in order to go to heaven, I would not go. So I never wanted to go swimming with the Nesters. Terry told me that I was part of the family and it would be good for me to go. So I went, but we agreed that I would not get into the water. We got to the swimming pool; I ended up getting in the water and I loved it.

There was a missionary fellowship once every month. All the missionaries would gather at a certain place to worship and eat together. I was still new in the Nester family. Even if they had treated me like family, I never thought they would take me to the missionary fellowship, especially since I was not officially adopted. The night of the missionary fellowship, everyone was getting ready to go out and I was lying on the bed. Terry came and asked why I was not getting ready, and I told him the missionary fellowship was just for missionaries and their families. He replied, "We are going together because you are our family, Emma."

We went to the missionary fellowship together, and at first I felt very uncomfortable because I had no idea what was going on. Some missionaries wondered why I was at the fellowship. Every time they asked, the Nesters came and said, "Emma is part of our family." The rest of the night went well. Since I was together with the Nesters, all the other missionaries at the fellowship treated me like I belonged there.

Terry was invited to speak at difference conferences, and whenever we were not in school, we all went out to the conferences as a family. But more than just going, we all ministered at these conferences. Mama Debbie usually sang right before Terry got up to speak, and she taught women. Jonah, Natalie and I spoke to the youth. Some of my very favorite moments in ministry were with the whole family.

My favorite memory was, when we went out to do ministry in one village, but Jonah and I broke off to go do hut-to-hut evangelism. We walked into a witch's compound. I was very scared because I knew how dangerous witches can be, and how much they hated the gospel. I tried to tell Jonah that we should go another direction, and Jonah said, "We have to do this together." So together we boldly walked into this man's compound. We asked if we could talk to him, and he granted us permission. To make a long story short, we shared the gospel with this man, and by the end of the day, his entire household received Christ.

I was a very shy boy back in then; standing up to speak before people was one thing I hated to do. Even at school when I had to do give an answer in class I was always shy. However, ministering together with the Nesters gave me a certain confidence that I never had before. Even going to talk to the witch doctor, I doubt if I would have gone to talk to him alone. But doing things together made it easier to minister, even in tough conditions.

My school time was not the same as Natalie and Jonah. Sometimes they were in school while I was on break; these are the times they stayed home with Mama Debbie, but Terry and I went out to do ministry. We travelled to distant villages together. We saw the worst of Uganda's roads together. He preached to the grownups, and I reached out to the young people and kids. God was using us to touch lives. One thing I miss most is doing ministry together with my family.

I have saved this one for last, because it was by far my favorite time together with the family. One Saturday morning we all went out to play baseball with other missionaries. Jonah, Natalie and I played while Terry and Mama Debbie came to interact with other missionaries. To that point, I had never played or watched baseball. But since it was something we were doing together as a family, I figured I would give it a shot.

We got to the field, and one of the missionaries told me how to hold the bat, how to hit the ball, how to play, and all the rules I needed to follow. I could not do all the other things well but I could run fast enough to get past all the stops. However, baseball was a boring sport to me. It was not like soccer; we kept stopping and it was not fun. Besides, I could not hit the ball well, so I just played for the sake of it, not competitively.

I was lucky enough this one time to I hit the ball correctly, and I started running to get to the next stop. But as I was running I heard Terry's voice loudly scream, "Come on son!!" This was very special because it was the very first time that he ever called me son. After being rejected, the thing I desired most was to be a son again. When I heard Terry say that it, meant the world to me.

Just that word "son" from Terry worked like a Red Bull that energized me; I went from running to flying Usain Bolt style. Boring baseball suddenly became so much fun. From that time on I played with so much vigor, and our team ended up winning. That day was so awesome, and I couldn't wait for the next chance to play baseball. Just like that, I started loving baseball.

Not too long after baseball, Terry was invited to speak at a conference. This time, Jonah and Natalie were in school, so just Terry and I went. The conference was at a vocational school so many young people were there. Terry introduced me as his son, and right after he spoke he invited me up to speak. I did a horrible job speaking but I was very happy Terry introduced me as son. Now I looked at him the same way I had looked at my father before.

During lunch break at the conference I walked around the school with Terry. While we walked I remembered moments, when I was about five years old, when I walked around so proudly with my biological father. I tried to walk like he did, and put my little feet in the footprints he left. At this moment I felt five all over again, following Terry like the excited little boy that I was at five. I tried to walk the same way Terry walked. I made the same jokes he made. Pastor Terry was slowly becoming my hero, not because he had superpowers. It was because he was filling the void of a father and a friend in my life, and he was doing an excellent job at it. He provided me with a family and loved me like a son, and this qualified him for hero status in my life. Whenever I interacted with the youth at the conference, I was so proud to talk about Terry. I was so glad to praise him, just like I would have done my father.

I learnt from the Nesters that togetherness is one of the most basic ingredients of a healthy family. My view changed. I learnt that family is not just a bunch of people under one roof. Rather, togetherness defines family. There is something sweet in doing things together, even it is crying; it's a different feeling when you cry together compared to crying alone. Rejoicing alone might also feel empty if you have to do it alone. Burdens are not as heavy if you carry them together. Family togetherness was the very first thing I tasted at the Nesters, and this principal will be with me for forever.

CHAPTER 15

A GROWN MAN CRYING

Spending time together every morning—eating, having devotions and praying together—opened my eyes to something about the Nesters I was not used to seeing. While sharing devotions and praying together, often times Pastor Terry broke down and started crying. One time we were reading through a Max Lucado devotional book that talked about the parent who asked to Jesus to heal his crippled son. Terry was crying by the time we finished the devotional. That was the first time I saw him cry during devotions, but it was not the last.

To me this was rather strange, because in my culture, men DO NOT cry. Crying was considered a very weak emotion, and I thought only females and babies cried. In Uganda, people have witnessed so much pain that death is an everyday thing. Children starving to death, people being killed, and all sorts of horrible things; Ugandans witnessed these things so often that it was no longer a big deal to see people die or get hurt. As a matter of fact many people did not cry at funerals anymore; they were more concerned with who will be the heir. People's heart had become very hard, even parents towards their children.

I was always surprised to see Terry deeply moved to tears when he saw starving little children on TV. I was not in tears, and I was a Christian, too. I was so used to seeing the street kids begging for food that I got used to it, and it never bothered me anymore, at least not to the point of tears.

So I never understood why Terry was in tears. I had never started crying just from read God's word.

I didn't understood why a grown man like Terry would cry, especially before us. But I came to learn, from the Nesters, that if a man loves and understands love, there are things that will make him cry. The Apostle Paul said, *"For I wrote you out of great distress and anguish of heart and with many tears, not to grieve you but to let you know the* depth of my love *for you" (2 Corinthians 2:4).* Terry was not weak. As a matter of fact he was a stronger and a bigger (I only mean muscles) man than many Ugandan men I knew. But Terry had a tender, loving heart, and because of it, some things brought tears to his eyes. José N. Harris, MI VIDA said, "Tears shed for another person are not a sign of weakness. They are a sign of a pure heart."

At first, watching Terry cry, confused me. But it was good to know that men, too, could express their emotions, and God was slowly softening my heart. One night during our time together, we watched the movie "Facing the Giants." As we watched the movie, there were scenes that touched my heart deeply, and caused me to cry. When Jonah turned around and saw tears in my eyes, I was ashamed because I expressed weak emotions. I had no idea what in the world was happening to me that I could cry over a movie.

This movie touched me most when it talked about love. I remember the scene where things were falling apart at work for the husband; he was coaching the high school football team. And at home his wife was going through pain of not being able to become pregnant. One night as she was talking to her husband, she broke down tears when she told him that she could not have a baby and "did not understand why she loved someone she had not yet met so much."

That scene made me cry, because at the Nester's, I was starting to understand and see what love looked like. Furthermore, somehow I associated with that woman when she wondered why she loved someone so much that she had even never met (if you keep reading you will find out why). The other scene that touched me was the disabled father who went so far to support his son. He was in a wheelchair and could not stand, but he still tried to get up on his feet to support his son.

He succeeded. Somehow he was able to stand up in his wheelchair, and he raised his hands in support for his son who was about to kick the ball. I was balling. Out of love for his son, this disabled man was willing to do what seemed impossible for a man in a wheelchair. I was beginning to understand love, and it left me in tears. There was a change taking place in my life. It felt strange to cry, but it also felt good to be moved by something.

The next time I went out on the streets, I did not look at the street kids in the same way as before. Somehow, my heart was filled with compassion for these children. This compassion opened my eyes to all the brokenness, pain and death in my country. This bothering me in a way it never had before, and sometimes it left me in tears. I actually began feeling a genuine love for my people. There were times when we went out for ministry, and upon seeing the suffering of the people in the village, I would break out in tears. Their pain touched my heart, and I hurt too.

All those times Terry cried during devotions finally made sense to me: when he talked about the depth of God's love for us, when he spoke of how much he loved his family, and when he talked about his love for the people to whom he came to minister. It made sense because I was starting to love and understand love. When I meditated on the goodness of God, how He loved me and all He had brought me through, I too was in tears. Sometimes I started crying from just listening to a worship song. I would cry when I went on my knees to pray to God.

I became a very different person from of the times I saw the Nesters cry. I learnt compassion. I started to care for people more. I started to understand people more. More importantly, I became a better lover. I believe that it is very important to get to the point of crying. Many times, tears on the outside are a proof of the compassion and love we feel on the inside for others.

I became a better minister after my heart was softened at the Nesters house. Love and compassion filled me. That is why, when I looked out and saw the brokenness in my country, it made me cry. This also gave me a stronger desire to take the gospel to these people. There was a new fire burning in me and love for my people that I had not felt before. There were moments I would read about child sacrifice in my country, and I was overwhelmed with distress and compassion. I cried, and these tears brought me to my knees in prayer for me country.

Crying is not weak. As a matter of fact, I see men of God in the Bible who wept.

"Then David and the people who were with him raised their voices and wept until they had no more strength to weep." (1 Samuel 30:4)

"Then Joseph fell on his father's face and wept over him and kissed him." (Genesis 50:1)

"'Now, O LORD, please remember how I have walked before you in faithfulness and with a whole heart, and have done what is good in your sight.' And Hezekiah wept bitterly." (2 Kings 20:3)

"While Ezra prayed and made confession, weeping and casting himself down before the house of God, a very great assembly of men, women, and children, gathered to him out of Israel, for the people wept bitterly." (Ezra 10:1)

"Jesus wept." (John 11:35)

"For I wrote to you out of much affliction and anguish of heart and with many tears, not to cause you pain but to let you know the abundant love that I have for you." (2 Corinthians 2:4)

I am convinced that tears should be part of our ministries. I will go a little further and say that, if we are going to be effective ministers, tears are necessary. All those biblical men of God, even Jesus Christ, were in tears on many different occasions as they ministered. Jesus wept when Lazarus died. He cried tears of sorrow for the hardened hearts of men and for the lost.

"And when [Jesus] drew near and saw the city, he wept over it, saying, 'Would that you, even you, had known on this day the things that make for peace! But now they are hidden from your eyes.'" (Luke 19:41-42)

I have heard many people say that the USA that was founded on God's standards. Yet, this country is trying so hard to remove God from the government and the country at large. The Supreme Court legalized same sex marriage (legalized sin). I read in the news of how many babies have been killed through abortion. I hear about shootings of children, like the one in Connecticut. In America and around the world, I see young people being shot every day. There are unjust wars. There are broken families, and many kids are growing up without a father. Human trafficking is worldwide; young girls are being sold and bought to be used as sex objects, men raping children. Joseph Kony of the Lord's Resistance Army, made child soldiers in Uganda. There are child sacrifices. And many people are dying in their sins every day.

If all those things above do not make us weep, then it is a shame. It means we are missing the heart of Christ. We have grown so used to sin that it does not bother us anymore. If we are going to change this world for Christ, we have to have the heart of Christ. The same things that made Christ weep ought to make us weep. When we look out into our cities our hearts ought to be broken. We ought to be sorrowful and distressed about the spiritual darkness in our cities.

Even the condition of the church should make us weep. If church has turned into a social club, and pastors have turned into entertainers, who say whatever people want to hear, this ought to make us cry. When we see churches where everything else is more important than Christ and the Word of God, it should distress us to tears. I am sure Christ weeps for the church, too. I believe that if we are genuinely concerned about winning souls for Christ, then the spiritual condition of the people will cause us to weep.

I will share a story of a man who had a genuine concern for his people. His name was Nehemiah. He said, "*Hanani, one of my brothers, came with certain men from Judah. And I asked them concerning the Jews who escaped, who had survived the exile, and concerning Jerusalem. And they said to me, 'The remnant there in the province who had survived the exile is in great trouble and shame. The wall of Jerusalem is broken down, and its gates are destroyed by fire.'" (Nehemiah 1:2-3)*

Nehemiah was the Persian king's cup-bearer. He lived with honor and riches and, simply put, life was a whole lot easier for him than his fellow Jews. Since he was doing well enough for himself, other people's distress could easily not concern him. Today, some people are starving to death, but many live as though it is not their problem. They're only concerned that their own family and dog are healthy and eating well. Even Nehemiah could have easily thought the other Jews brought their suffering upon themselves when they disobeyed God. This was the consequence for their sin. A lot of us think this way. Sometimes we are not concerned about those people who are hurting because we think they are simply suffering because of their sins.

Nehemiah, however, was very concerned for these Jews; that is why he asked about them. Henani and the other men told him the problem; his fellow Jews were being afflicted, and the walls of Jerusalem were broken down. Let me pause to explain the significance of Jerusalem's wall. In this period of time, without a wall, a city was nothing more than a group of people waiting to be robbed, harassed and even killed. The wall served as protection for the entire city. So, without the complete wall, the people were in constant danger. The broken city walls and burned gates were a constant reminder of the humiliation to which their captors had subjected them.

To Nehemiah, the Jews' problem was clear. If we are going to be broken for our people first we have to come to that realization that there is a problem. We can see this even by the news we read about death, human trafficking, child abuse, violence, and other injustice in our world. When we realize that there is a problem, it should concern us. Before I stay with the Nesters, I had grown so accustomed to the problems in my country that I acted like the problems were not there, and they never concerned me.

Do you see that there are problems around you, especially spiritual problems? Do you see broken families? Do you realize the number of unborn babies that are killed every day? Do all these still count as problems to you? Or are you so used to them that you do not think of them as problems?

If we see the problems, as believers in Christ, we need to respond to them. How did Nehemiah respond to his problem? Verse four says, "And it came to pass, when I heard these words, that I sat down and wept, and mourned certain days, and fasted, and prayed before the God of heaven."

The first thing Nehemiah did, after hearing the news, was to sit down. Have you ever received horrible news that sucks the energy out of you and forces you to sit down for a moment? My friend, Reggie Smith, called me one time to give me some bad news. The first thing he said was, *"Hey E, I hope you are sitting down, because this is bad."* I think Nehemiah sat down because this news was so bad. After he sat down, he started to weep. He wept out of compassion and concern that a pagan nation was attacking not only the Jews, but also their God. Nehemiah was so sorrowful that he mourned for days, but his sorrow was not going to help if it was his only response. Nehemiah recognized the problem, it distressed him, and now he decided to do something about the problem. To find a solution, he prayed to God.

It is common today that we will see problems that distress us, but we are not willing to do anything about them. We are waiting for the next Martin Luther King, the government, or the pastors to solve them. The only thing we do very well is sit and whine about things. There are people in church complaining about why the church is not doing a number for things. Instead, I want to ask them, "Why don't you take the lead?"

I heard a story about a big boulder in the middle of a road. Many people saw it, and it bothered them. They made statements like, "What on earth is happening?" "Why is a boulder in the way?" It made them angry, and they wondered why someone didn't just move it. This boulder simply bothered and made them mad. However, one man saw the boulder, and he grabbed a big stick and he started slowly to move the rock. Beneath the boulder was a note that said, "Thank you for serving. Many have passed, complained and continued on, but you have been concerned enough to do something."

The lesson I learnt from the Nesters has been very important in my ministry. I learnt love and compassion, which was expressed outward through my tears. My eyes were opened to see that there was a problem, and the problem distressed me to tears. And the tears pushed me to find a solution. Like Nehemiah, I run to God, because He can fix everything and anything. Nothing is impossible with Him.

CHAPTER 16

THE NESTERS LOVED ME

My heart was going through a reformat, and new software was being downloaded onto my system. It was the software of love and compassion. I had been a Muslim for fourteen years, and a lot had been downloaded in my head. Love was the only thing that could remove all the evil I had learnt during those first years. At the Nesters, I was in the right place; my heart was getting a transformation. First I started feeling compassion, and then I learnt love from the way the Nesters showed and expressed it to one another.

I was very shocked one morning when I walked into the kitchen and saw Terry, the head of the family, (in Uganda we say "the big drum") cooking something. This shocked me because, in my country, men barely ever enter the kitchen, let alone cook something. I never saw my father cook anything, not even boil water. In many cases if you see a Ugandan man get into the kitchen at home to cook, his wife might be getting the boot soon. Some men have more than one wife, so that if one is not able to cook, they will just go to the other wife for the meals. It is almost a shameful thing for a man to be in the kitchen cooking.

Mama Debbie was not sick, so part of me thought their marriage might be going south. When I talked to Terry, though, he told me that he cooked because he loved his wife. He wished to give her a break from the kitchen. The people we love we often give gifts. Terry gave Debbie the gift of time away from the kitchen to relax. I was very impressed, because I had not seen this before. I learnt a very important lesson that will forever live in my heart. Love is not just the three little words (I love you). It is the actions that follow.

Terry was teaching me knew things that many Ugandan men never do. He often cried, and now he was in the kitchen cooking. Mom was very happy to take time away from the kitchen to just relax at home, read a book or hang out with her friends. I told Mom that one day I want to make my wife happy in the same way Terry was making her happy, especially in the kitchen. I developed a desire to cook, however I was the worst cook I knew. Putting bread in the toaster and boiling eggs was the best I ever did, and even with that I came up short on many occasions.

I often watched Mom closely when she cooked. I peeled potatoes for her and chopped onions and tomatoes. I had not gotten a chance to cook for anyone, even though I wanted to practice what I saw Mom do. Finally, the perfect opportunity came when, one day, the Nesters travelled to Kampala to take Jonah and Natalie to the dentist. At home it was just me and the young man, Daniel, who worked in the yard. Right after the Nesters drove outside the gate, I told Daniel that I would be the cook for the day. I preferred to practice my cooking on Daniel rather than my wife. If the food did not kill Daniel or make him sick, then my practice would have been a success.

I went to the freezer and grabbed some chicken breasts. The menu for the day was going to be Emma's special fried chicken. Daniel asked me if I was sure about what I was doing. I told him I had acquired enough experience from watching Mom cook. I opened the spice cabinet, and found at least fifty spices. I had no idea what was what. So I decided to just mix about ten spices that caught my eye and hope for the best. I was already feeling like Mama Debbie because I had her apron on and I liked the sound when I threw stuff in the hot oil in the frying pan. I fried the chicken and soon it looked brown and ready to eat.

I went outside as Mama Debbie usually does, and in the same tone, I yelled, "Daniel, honey, lunch is ready!!" Daniel said, "Ok Mom. I will be there shortly." Daniel came in, and though the chicken looked good, and he was excited to eat. However, his excitement died immediately after one bite of Emma's special chicken. The chicken had all sorts of tastes on the top and the inside was still frozen. I missed one very important step while I was cooking. I forgot that you do not take the chicken out of the freezer and immediately throw it onto the frying pan. Mama Debbie used to let it thaw out before she would cook it. I thought the heat would unfreeze the chicken. I was so wrong.

I had to pretend like I liked my cooking, but it was the most horrible chicken ever cooked. Thank goodness, there was always a way out. It was called peanut butter and jelly sandwich or chocolate cereal. When Mom came home, Daniel made sure he told her how I almost killed him with my cooking. From that moment I was excused from all cooking duties. I would volunteer to cook and everyone would say things like, "I am not really hungry anymore," or "We still want to live," or "Alert the ambulance!" That is how much they liked my cooking.

Very recently, at a prayer breakfast at my church, one of the deacons gave me the duty of making gravy. I made it and called it Ugandan Gravy. By the next morning Sunday, half the men who came to prayer breakfast were all sick. The next time I asked if the deacon needed help making gravy, he joked that we didn't want to make people sick at church. I still love learning to cook when I get a chance, because someday I want to show love to my wife in the same way Terry did.

Debbie and Terry expressed their love to each other and also to us. I do not remember going a single day without hearing "I love you" from the Nesters. At first I thought to myself, "Jeez these people say 'I love you' way too much." It gave me goose bumps, especially when it was said to me, because I was not used to it. It was so hard for me to say those words like they did. When one of the Nesters said "I love you" to me, it was easier to say "Thank you" rather than "I love you, too." And sometimes I would say "Me too." I was not used to it, and it didn't feel right deep within me.

Natalie, Jonah and I were not the best kids by a long shot. But the crazy thing was, even while we were messing up, we still got to hear "I love you." On the phone I knew exactly what the last line was going to be. For most of the time I have known the Nesters, before they hang up the phone, they say, "I love you honey." Or "son" or "sweetie." In one month at the Nesters, I heard those words more than I had heard them in fourteen years. This had a tremendous impact on my life.

Sometimes they did not even need to say the words "I love you," because the way they talked screamed it. Mama Debbie always used words like honey, sweetie, cupcake, and pumpkin. I had no idea what some of them meant. But through those words I saw how much she loved us. I enjoyed being in her sight because she always said something beautiful. Formerly, if someone called me "pumpkin" I probably would have started a fight. We enjoyed insulting each other more than showing love in our speech. But now I knew she called me these sweet names because she loved me. As she would say, *"I love the snort out of you, Emma."*

Countless times I walked into the house, and I saw Terry hugging Jonah or Natalie, or Debbie hugging or kissing Terry, or the family just playing around to show affection for each other. They would buy each other little gifts, for no special occasion. They wrote each other little notes saying "I love you." As a matter of fact, Terry told me this note-writing has been going on for a long time. He had written and received letters from Debbie since they started dating. He had a special box where he kept them. When they were preparing to move to Uganda, he opened the special box that, by now, was full of all the love letters. Reading through a couple of letters made him cry as he thought about how much Debbie loved him.

Before, I had only watched these things in movies. Things in movies are not really true, so I had no idea that people could love like this in real life. This was my first time seeing it. I started to believe in love on higher level, and I wanted to love like the Nesters loved. With the love we all received there was real happiness at home. Yes, there were some struggles, but we loved each other through those struggles. Even when I fought with Jonah on the basketball court, at the end of the day he would walk into the room and say, *"I love you Emma."* It became so important for me to hear those words.

At first I never saw the need to say, "I love you," because I assumed people I loved already knew it. I knew that I loved them, so I did not want to waste time repeating myself. I guess that is how my parents thought, too. Later on it was not that I assumed they knew. I just took some people for granted and I stopped telling them. My parents provided me shelter, school fees and food; these were legitimate reasons for me to assume they loved me, and I never need them to say those words. But after living with the Nesters I learnt that our loved ones do need to hear it.

We live in a broken, mean world that is run by the devil. It might be that the only things the world tells our loved ones are: "You are ugly," "You are dumb," You are nobody," and "You do not matter." They need to hear about our love for them! It is easy for people to be evil and rude. When I was out on the streets, I was called an infidel and a stupid boy. Those three little words, "I love you," became the most important words I heard after long days away from home. When you say "I love you," those might be the only positive words your loved ones get to hear all day. Hearing those words might be the best part of their day, the only thing worth smiling about. We can light up someone's day simply by letting them know we love them.

In school, I was that short little boy that students laughed. They made fun of my big nose, they thought I had a big head, and I was ugly. When I spoke, many thought that I was slow. No girls liked me, and I was not as athletic as the other students on the basketball team. I was not the best in class either. For a moment it felt like the whole world was against me, and I was no good. I needed reassurance that, even if it felt like the world was against me, there were still people that loved and treasured me. By hearing the words "I love you, Emma," I was reassured that I might not be good enough for the people at school, but I was good enough at home. That is what kept me going.

God taught me that our loved ones shouldn't to assume we love them. They need to see it, hear it, and feel it. I heard of a mother who read a bedtime story to her daughter, kissed her goodnight, turned off the light, and she was heading out. Before she left, her daughter stopped her and said, "Mom, would you sleep with me tonight?" The mother asked the daughter why, and she said that she was scared the monster would attack her during the night.

"Baby," Mother said, "I prayed for you and you know Jesus loves you and He will protect you." The little girl replied, "Mom I know Jesus will protect me, but I need Jesus here with skin on him." That little girls believes Jesus will protect her, but she is at a point where she needs to see hear and feel Jesus right there. Sometimes we can be "Jesus with skin on" for people in our lives. Many of us know that we are loved, but still we need to hear, see and feel that love. That might be reason the Bible, over and over again, reminds us of how much God loves us.

The problem for me was that, while sometimes I assumed that my parents or friends loved me, other times I assumed they did not love me. Hearing it would have helped me out a lot. And when I assumed they didn't love me, I went to find love somewhere else. I think part of the reason some girls go with men who say they love them is simply because they are yearning to hear those lovely words. I have heard friends say, "We know men lie." Still, they fall for or live with the lies, because of how these men verbally express love to them. Many people use media, like public chat rooms, to find those expressions of love.

I have come to realize that there is nothing as important as receiving and giving love. Jesus summed up all the commandments in the Bible in just two commands; love the Lord your God, and love your neighbor as you love yourself. Paul, in *1 Corinthians 13*, also recognizes that the greatest gift is love. Everybody needs love, everybody is looking for love, and everybody needs to feel love. I learnt that we have constant opportunities to love, with our words and actions, to our loved ones. But when we miss out on those opportunities, other voices in the world will rise up. When we fail to tell our young girls we love them, pimps and men with bad motives might tell them. Gangs might tell our young boys they love them.

Going back home from school was always exciting, because most of what I heard there was love. This was quite a change from living with my biological father. Sometimes I would rather stay out late and come back home when my father was already in bed. Being around him was not an exciting thing, because I heard more negativity than love. I heard a lot about the things I did wrong and nothing about what I did right. It felt like he was more interested in my mistakes than in the right things I did. I had friends in the dorms who hated going home, just because they never felt love at home.

People cannot give what they do not have. The reason it was so hard to say "I love you" to the Nesters was that I had never previously been given that "I love you" gift. It was much easier to give anger. Jonah knows this part of me very well. I was very capable of saying hurtful words, yet very uncomfortable with saying "I love you." But as I heard love more often from the Nesters, it became easier for me to speak love. Love is the most inexpensive gift we can give each other. Parents, spare your children the wonder and insecurity of feeling unloved. Instead, help mold for them a lifetime of security. When it comes to love, say it and live it.

From what I have written above, it mostly sounds like Mom and Dad gave us love, but it was not a one way street. We had to let them know that we loved them too. It's important for parents to let their kids know they love them, but it is equally important for the kids to return the favor to their parents. Whenever we told Mom and Dad we loved them, they felt good. It was one reward for all the work and energy and love they put in raising us. They felt appreciated and like they were doing a good job in raising us.

So parents, children and friends, do not neglect telling your loved ones that you do love them. Those words are able to convey so much more than you can imagine. They have power to heal, renew, uplift, and comfort. They can instill hope, warm hearts and calm people. Therefore, not telling our loved ones that we love them might be similar to keeping medicine from a sick person.

Pastor Terry used to say, "Do not say hateful words to people, because that might be the last time you see them. Every time you get a chance, speak love." Relationships and people die. Life ends, and the time will come when you can no longer say, "I love you" to those people. A time may come when you will never again hear those words. Maybe you waited too long, maybe you were busy with work and life. Maybe you hesitated when you should have said it, maybe you assumed the other person knew, and now you have missed out on the chance to actually say it. As your loved one leaves for work, that might be the last time they ever walk through that door.

You may end up living a life of regret, wishing you used the opportunity to let them know you your love. Do they see more of your anger and disappointment in them or your love for them? Do they know you love them? If you never say it, you will never really know.

We have a chance right now. We are not assured of tomorrow. Therefore, when you have a chance now to tell someone you love them, take it. Do not wait till they are in the hospital about to die. Do not wait because and then live wishing you had done differently.

I had been through so much pain, hate, and rejection that really crushed my heart. The only thing that healed me and made me whole again was love—God's love and the love I received from the Nesters. When I came home from school and Mom said, "I love you Emma," to me it meant that she believed in me, cared for me, and was there for me. It meant that she valued me, understood me, treasured me and did not hate me. That was all I needed. As long as I had God and the Nesters, the whole world could have been against me and I would have been alright.

I used to see a TV commercial for detergent. A kid came home with very dirty clothes, but his mom soaked the dirty clothes in detergent and they came out spotless. When I was at the Nester's home, I felt like I was constantly being soaked in love. At the end of it, all the dirt that I had picked up from my Muslim years began to wash away. For the first time, I actually looked Terry in the face and I told him that I loved him. I never felt uneasy or had a single goose bump. I was in tears right after I told him that.

As I watched how Terry loved Debbie and his kids, I developed a very deep desire to have a family of my own in the future. I desired to be able to love them the same way. My desire changed from growing up and becoming rich to growing up and having a happy family that I love above everything else. I want to have money to support my family. However money is not my dream, the only thing I really dream about, that keeps me excited about the future, is that sometime, God-willing, I will have a wife and children that I will love and cherish just like Terry loved Debbie and his kids. A lot of things went wrong with my biological family. However I feel like I can correct those things by being better with my own family.

When I saw how happy everyone was in the Nester family because of the love we shared, I wanted to love. I wanted to make someone happy, and I wanted someone to be able to say, "Emmanuel truly loves me." I desired that, when I leave earth, people would say, "Emmanuel was a man who loved." From that time on I was driven by love. Though I had not met my wife yet, at that moment, I fell in love with her. During that time I started praying for her and our family. When I went to sleep, I started dreaming about my future family.

I would lock my door and write to that special someone out there. I wrote notes like, "Dear you, we have not met yet, but I would like to let you know that I have been thinking about you today, I can't wait for the moment when I finally lay eyes on you." "Today I prayed for you." Do you remember the scene, in "Facing the Giants," that made me cry? When the coach's wife said, "I do not know why I love someone so much that I have never met," she was talking about the baby she wanted to have. I cried because I understood exactly what she was talking about.

I still eagerly wait for that day when I get to let this love bomb explode for my wife. I could summarize my entire relationship with the Nesters in this way: I was loved, and I learnt how to love. I learnt to love God better, to love people on a whole new level, and to love my (future) wife unconditionally. Of everything that happened, the most important was love. This is the best gift anyone ever gave me.

CHAPTER 17

THE NESTERS TREASURED ME

My friend Jacob and his wife were expecting their first baby. They went into the hospital for an ultrasound and they left with the sonograms. Jacob was very excited about the sonograms. He showed me pictures and posted some on Facebook. He asked me, "Isn't she beautiful?" To me, however, there was nothing beautiful about that sonogram. As a matter of fact I had no idea what I was looking at. It looked like a black and white landscape photograph. To Jacob it was not merely a picture. For him, that sonogram showed a very precious treasure, and that made it beautiful.

It was not so much the sonogram that excited him, but the promise of a precious baby in his wife's womb. It would have been a different story if the picture showed no baby but only his wife's organs. This baby was precious to Jacob. I felt precious at the Nester's because of how much they treasured me. I was by no means beautiful, physically or spiritually. I came up short on very many occasions, but the Nester's looked at the promise of a beautiful Emma through God's work. They did not look at what I used to be, or what I was, but what I was going to be through God's grace, and that is what made me precious.

Mom liked to decorate the house with all sort of things. On the front door, she hung a flower and a piece of wooden art. It was shaped like a heart and said "Welcome." She had gotten it recently and she loved it. She put it at the front door so all visitors would see it. One day I was in the front yard shooting baskets. The basketball hoop was not far from the front door. For some reason, probably because I missed all my shots, I got upset and kicked the ball in the air. I didn't mean to kick it in the direction of the front door, but when the ball left my foot, that is exactly where it went. The next thing I heard was the sound of Mom's precious art hitting the floor in pieces.

A few seconds later, as I stood there puzzled, the front door opened. Natalie was the first one to come see what that noise was. Natalie looked at me, and all she said was, "You are a dead man." I really wished I was dreaming. I was very scared. I knew how much Mom loved that art piece, how many of her friends visited and told her it was so beautiful, and how often she would just stare at it. Natalie closed the door, and we tried to see if we could glue it back together. We could not. Then the door opened again, and the next person on the scene was Mom.

The moment I laid my eyes on Mom I was thinking, *this is it. The next conversation I am going to have will be with the Apostle Paul or King David.* I was that scared. Then Mom asked, "What happened?" I tried to speak, but I was so scared that words would not even come out of my mouth. So Natalie tried to explain what happened. Mom stooped down and looked at her art piece. Then she glanced at me, and saw how scared I was, so much so that I was literally trembling. Holding a piece of the art in her hand, she stood up again and looked at me. I was wishing the ground would swallow me. Then Mom called me to herself, but I was thinking, nope*! I am smarter than that, you are going to have to chase me around.* So I stayed still. Then again she said, "Honey come here," but I still didn't move. So she came closer to me, and as I was about to run, she said, "Honey, it is just an art piece."

For a minute, I thought my mind was playing tricks with me. I thought Mom was saying some angry things to me but my mind was totally changing her words. But it was reality. Mom said, "It is okay, honey. We can get another art piece." When I looked over at Natalie, she was as surprised as I was. This is not what we imagined was going to happen. Natalie then said to me, "Kid, you are precious. Mom loves you!" In the few words Mom said, she was simply telling me, "Emma you are more precious to me than a piece of art." I have heard of parents who have beat kids to death over material things that the parents consider precious. That was one of the few times I my life that I felt really treasured.

Debbie Nester taught me how to deal graciously with others, especially after they make a mistake. She taught me that day that accidents happen, even when we least expect them. While she hated that her art piece was broken, she knew it was not my desire to break it. Then the word she said right after the incident showed me how much value she attached to me and to the art. I felt that I was more precious than that art piece. It is no joke when I tell you that I have heard of parents in my country who have killed their children because they broke the television or the radio. I learnt that day that I was precious to Debbie. Through that, God was also teaching me that I was even more precious to Him. In fact all people are precious to God. Therefore since all people are precious to God, we should treat others as the precious people they are.

Not long before I moved in with the Nesters, my family and friends saw no value in me. I was deemed useless to my family and the Muslim community at large. The wild cats in the village were of more value than me. Some said that I did not even deserve to live. I was a reject, not only to the Muslims but also to some Christians. I was not the smartest in class, not the best on the soccer team, and I was far from being the best looking young man around. There was nothing special about me to make me feel precious. So I walked around thinking I was not worth much. I had become a Christian and a son of the Most High, but I was still living like a slave. I was still living like more of a burden than a treasure. However, that day, through Debbie Nester, God taught me that I was His precious treasure. I learnt that God did not look at me as a slave, a sinner, a reject, a burden, or a short, unattractive Ugandan boy. He looked at me as His son, His chosen one, as the apple of His eye.

I learnt that I was precious, but I felt like God was teaching me this lesson not so I could feel good about myself and move on with my life, but so I could teach and treat others like they are precious too. I learnt that, in the same way Mom graciously treated me, I should treat others. At the Nesters, I started owning things that I had never dreamt of having. I had an MP3 player, a lot more money, new clothes, and much more than what many students had. Slowly I started to treasure the things I owned. I loved my MP3 player and all the new clothes Jonah gave me. In the dorms a student stole some of my good stuff, and I found out later that it was one of my friends. I was very angry, but I remembered the time I broke Mom's art piece. So I told this young man that I could report him, make him pay me back or have him expelled from school, but that he was more precious to me and to God than all the materials he stole. Later, I shared the gospel with him, he became a believer and we became even closer friends.

There are a lot of good products out there—cars, electronics and even money—that it is so easy for us today to be very materialistic. It is so easy to view the things we own or want as being more precious than people. I have read many news articles about people killing because of money, cars or land. I have heard of churches where, though people are spiritually dying, they are more committed to making the church buildings more sophisticated that to helping people grow spiritually. Many churches are very concerned about buying the best quality sound systems and new carpet, while people within the church are going without food. People are dying in their sins every day, but we spend money on sophisticating our churches instead of investing in missions. The carpets, the church buildings, the sounds system and the lights are all great things, but when we give them first priority and treat them more precious than people for whom Christ died, we are wrong. Sometime the whole church will become so entangled in the material issues that they are about to split. But then few or no people will be concerned enough to go visit a sick church member who is in the hospital.

That might be the reason we have a lot of fancy, nice looking churches, but very few believers. It might be because we have attached more value to all these things at the expense of people. In such churches there are more leadership meetings to talk about beautifying, expanding and improving the church buildings and very few meetings about how church can reach out and serve the people and take the Gospel out. But it would be very sad, at the end of it all, to present a resume to Christ that says, "I built a very beautiful church, I had the best sound systems, and the church was fully air conditioned." All these things will not matter, because Christ commissioned us to make disciples of all nations, not to build sophisticated churches. The main problems people are going through today will not be solved by a beautiful church, a great sound system or any other material possession. The solution is Christ, so we need to take the love of Christ to these people. However, unless we go back to the basics and realize that people are precious, we will not feel the need to love these people or share the love of God with them.

I do realize that it might be hard to treasure some people; we might not be very close to them, or there may be other reasons. But even when we fail to do that, we must treat all people like they are precious to God. "For God so loved the world, that he gave his only Son, that whoever believes in him should not perish but have eternal life." (John 3:16)

If we understand just how precious people are to God, maybe those famous television evangelists will stop spending so much time trying to get rich and spend more time drawing people to God. Preachers have attached very little value to people if they just want them for their money, or if they tell them messages that sound good to their ears but in the end lead them to destruction.

People are precious to God regardless of what they look like, where they came from or what they own. Christ did not die only for certain people but for all. I stop to look back at the people in my life that I thought were very annoying, very dumb, very arrogant, and very rude; all of those people are precious to God. I too was stupid, evil and lost in my sins, destined for eternity in hell. However, God saw me as precious enough that He came down and lifted me from my brokenness, and He created something beautiful out of me. He made me a royal priesthood.

I have friends that have left the church simply because the body of Christ attached less value to them. Rather than being treasured in the house of God, they have been judged, condemned and treated like they do not deserve to be there. People are looking for a place they feel valued and loved, but when they do not find that in church, some look for it in the world. And I know it would be a wrong motive to go to Church just to feel loved and valued, but again that is one way people see the love of Christ in our churches, the way we love and value each other. I watched a documentary recently about human trafficking. A young lady who, by the way, grew up going to church said she was loyal to her pimp because he was the only person in the world that ever treated her like she was precious and loved her. He was clearly using her, and she was willing to do whatever he asked because she felt like he treasured her.

When I think about the sacrifice God made to draw us to Himself, I get a glimpse of how precious we are to the Father. This pushes me to love people better and seek to draw them to Christ. Yes even the non-believers, Muslims, Buddhists, cult members and atheists are precious in God's eyes. God sent His only Son to die on the cross for them too. I have been guilty of judging non-believers on occasions. I have called them names, hated them and even avoided them. It has always been hard for me to look at these people as precious to God because it looks like they rebel against God. But still God calls me to look at them as people precious to Him.

"Now while Paul was waiting for them at Athens, his spirit was provoked within him as he saw that the city was full of idols." (Acts 17:16). Other translations say that Paul's spirit was troubled or distressed or stirred. Paul was distressed, but not because he was better than these people. He knew these people were precious before God too, yet they were going the wrong direction. As a devout follower of Jesus, idols in this city could have made Paul very sick. Maybe he could have done what most of us do, by telling these people they were going to hell.

As a Pharisee, who knew the law, Paul probably knew how seriously God hated and dealt with the sin of idol worship. Paul could have passed judgment on these people, but despite their sins, Paul knew that these people were still precious before God. Instead of feeling disgust and anger, he felt distress and compassion for them.

"So he reasoned in the synagogue with the Jews and the devout persons, and in the marketplace every day with those who happened to be there" (Acts 17:17). "Reasoning" here means that Paul explained the truth of the Gospel to

these people. I think Paul took an important step because I believe that when we come to the understanding how God values those around us, our response changes from judging and condemning them to pointing them to God. That is what Paul did.

All people are precious to God, regardless of what they did or are doing wrong. And it is God's desire for us believers to let people know that they are precious before God and He desires to have a relationship with them. But we are living in a world that rejects God. Despite sharing the truth about God's incredible love for them, many might resist or have no interest in God. At times I have given up on sharing God's love with such people. But God has not given up on them. God causes it to rain on the just and unjust. He gives them life, and every day that they get to walk on the face of this earth is a sign that God has not given up on them. This teaches me not to give up on anyone, but to keep pointing them to God.

Jesus knew that the very people who hurled insults at him, flogged Him, falsely accused Him and hung Him to the cross were precious to God. That is why even at the point when He experienced excruciating pain, he could still say, *"Father, forgive them, for they know not what they do" (Luke 23:34).*

When Paul reasoned with the people in Athens, he met some opposition. "Some of the Epicurean and Stoic philosophers also conversed with him. And some said, 'What does this babbler wish to say?' Others said, *'He seems to be a preacher of foreign divinities'—because he was preaching Jesus and the resurrection" (Acts 17:18).* Basically they called him a babbly fool. Paul did not quit. It was hard to still proclaim the truth to these people but it was worth it, because Paul knew what God thought about them and what God had done for them.

You would not be wrong to point out that these people were evil. You might be justified in calling them cultic, fools, sinners, wicked or idol worshippers. You could call them all that if you are going to base your words on their actions, but Paul's address to these people was based, not on their actions, but on God's thoughts. They were precious to God. I sense respect when Paul addressed them as *"Men of Athens."* We tend to identify people by their actions, but Paul addressed them with dignity. In verse 22, we see that Paul does not bash their gods, but he respects the fact that these men were also religious. It is very hard for Muslims to receive the gospel if we keep calling them terrorists. It would be rather insulting if you started sharing the gospel with a Buddhist by pointing out Buddha is just a fat man's statute.

"For as I passed along and observed the objects of your worship, I found also an altar with this inscription, 'To the unknown god.' What therefore you worship as unknown, this I proclaim to you" (Acts 17:23). Paul took the time to observe what they were worshipping, and when the opportunity came, he shared about the God who was unknown to the men of Athens, yet known to Paul. Ultimately, some people accepted the gospel and received Christ. Though some people rejected Paul's message, the most important thing is that Paul obeyed God and some people came to know the savior that day.

Jesus died for the Buddhists, Muslims, atheists, people on death row, the poor, the rich: everyone. God saw everyone as precious and still does. So we should let all men know that regardless of what they did they are precious to God, precious enough that he sent his Only Son to die on the cross for our sins.

I was evil, I was rebelling against God, and I hated Christians. I fought Christians and did what pleased me and my Muslim community at the expense of the Most High God. Still, God considered me precious. He kept calling me to follow Him and kept loving me. After I became a believer I did not become a complete package yet. I struggled with anger. In fact I had deep-seated anger toward Americans from all those years of being a Muslim. I had been taught that America was the enemy. Sometimes I did not obey Terry and Debbie. I got into constant fights with Jonah. There were some things Americans considered wrong, but in Uganda we considered alright; I kept doing those things and hurt the Nesters. Even now I am not a complete package, I sin every day, but yet God still treasures me. In the same way the Nesters treasured me despite of me. That forever changed how I treat other people.

CHAPTER 18

THE NESTER'S SPOKE LIFE INTO MY LIFE

"Of all the weapons of destruction that man could invent, the most terrible-and the most powerful-was the word. Daggers and spears left traces of blood; arrows could be seen at a distance. Poisons were detected in the end and avoided. But the word managed to destroy without leaving clues" (Paulo Coelho, The Fifth Mountain).

Words can be weapons of destruction, but if used properly, words have power to build up. They have tremendous power to plant seeds of love, happiness, confidence and success. "*Gracious words are like a honeycomb, sweetness to the soul and health to the body" (Proverbs 16:24).*

I was very blessed that God put me in a home where I heard beautiful words that were sweetness to my soul and health to my bones. I have never been with people whose words edified me like the Nesters. Starting from the mornings, it was such a joy to wake up. Mom was always up before us and she greeted us with beautiful words: good morning sweetheart, baby, honey, sunshine, pumpkin, cupcake, darling, and many more. Hearing words like these every morning, I started off my days with a smile.

For the first time in my life, I heard an elder say "please" and "sorry" to a young person because of the Nesters. I grew up in a culture where the elders were right and the young people were wrong. The elders commanded young people to do things, never asking politely or saying "please." When

I first started living with the Nesters, I would say things like, "Give me this," and Terry would hold onto it until I said "please." And "sorry" was one of the hardest words to get out of my mouth. I was used to arguing to convince the other person that I was right, even when I was wrong. When Terry said, "Pass me the salt, please," I was shocked. I wondered why he was saying "please" to me; he was older, richer, more educated and a way better person than I was. Yet he said "please" to me, not once or twice, but countless times.

When Terry, an American and far better person, said "sorry" to me, it felt like a king stepped down from his throne to come hang out with a commoner. This unlocked something in me. Now I did not just fear Terry as an older person, but I respected him for his humility. I looked at Terry as a friend, too. I became very comfortable talking to him. I trusted him. I was very free and more relaxed around him than I had even been with anyone of his age. After Terry said "please" to me, learning to be polite and say "please" to other became a very easy lesson to learn. As I made this word a part of my daily vocabulary, I quickly discovered that people responded better to politeness than to coldness.

Once, when we were playing basketball, Jonah, Terry and I were on the same team. We lost the game, and Terry came over to Jonah and me. He said "I am sorry I was not shooting well." This was totally new. My dad never said "sorry" to me. Elders very rarely, if ever, said sorry to young people. They instead made excuses to cover up their mistakes, or they simply ignored them. Terry and Debbie constantly said "sorry" to us. The easiest thing for all of us to do is to sin, against God or each other, but the hardest thing to do is acknowledge our faults and say we're sorry. Like I said, it was very hard for me to say "sorry," but by watching Terry and Debbie easily say it to us or each other, it became easier for me to say.

When my Muslim friends did something wrong, they often said, "I am only human." By this they meant, "I make mistakes" or "I am going to make mistakes." Saying this was a lot easier than saying I am sorry. Other times, if someone demanded an apology, a common response was, "Do not judge me because you are not perfect either." Sometimes we gave up on a relationship instead of apologizing and fixing it. I have seen marriages broken, friends turned into enemies, and relatives stop talking to each other. Sadly, much of this could have been fixed with the words "I'm sorry."

Hearing people like Debbie and Terry apologize to a teenager, like me, was so meaningful and instructive for me. I saw that they valued and respected me, because apologizing did not always mean they were wrong and I was right. It meant they valued me and our relationship more than their egos. This changed my heart. I had previously looked at saying the word "sorry" as evidence of weak character, but I was wrong. It takes a lot of strength to say that word. My relationship with everyone at home improved once I truly learnt how to say "I'm sorry."

Before I was learnt the important lesson of apologizing, sometimes I would fight with members of my family. Regardless of who was wrong, I would give that person the silent treatment for a day. In the end, though, the only thing that brought us back to talking terms was saying "sorry." I loved the Nesters, and I knew that apologizing was something I needed to get used to. As I look back, I recognize relationships I lost which could have been saved if I just apologized.

The Nesters loved to joke. They often said things that made everyone laugh and have a good time. One of my favorites were the tongue twisters, like "She sells seashells by the seashore" and "Rubber baby buggy bumpers." It was fun because, for some reason, I could not say these the way they said them. They often tried to have me say the tongue twisters because I sounded very funny.

I wanted to learn how to say "Rubber baby buggy bumpers," so I practiced by myself often. One time I was in the kitchen and did not know Mom was right behind me, as I was trying to practice. I totally got it wrong, and I think she was trying to be quiet, but she could not help but burst into laughter. Another time I was out cleaning the yard as I practiced, and this time I felt like I had nailed it. So I dropped the rake and ran into the house yelling for Mom to come quickly. She came, wondering what the problem was, but I told her I have something to tell you Mom! "Rubber baba bagga bumpers." Again she just burst into laughter.

I decided it was not working to practice on my own, so I had Natalie help me. This time, I finally had it nailed down. I practiced, and I was 105% sure I was not going to get it wrong this time. We were around the dinner table that night, and it was Moms birthday. After everyone had finished presenting their birthday gifts to Mom, I told her that I had a gift. She couldn't see or touch it, so I asked her to listen carefully. Then I said, "Rubber baby buggy bumpers … Happy birthday, Mom." I told her I that I had worked on this gift for a month till it was perfect to be presented to her. It was a fun night everyone clapped for me after I finally figured out that tongue twister. Natalie looked at me as if to say, "I am proud of you student." The good thing was, now that I had learnt how to say it, it was my turn to laugh at other Ugandans who would make mistakes if they tried to say it.

Terry always stressed saying positive words instead of negative words. Also, if I was angry, he would tell me not to say anything. When someone said "whatever" in a negative way, Terry always asked, "What if Jesus said 'whatever' to you?" I would say something negative, but in reply Mom would say, "I love you, too." I never heard Terry or Debbie curse. One time I was very angry, so I cursed. I expected Mom to understand, because she knew exactly why I was angry and that I was right in being angry. However, she did not approve of my language. She said, "In this house we do not use that kind of language, regardless of how angry you are. I told her I only said that because I was mad, and she replied, "If you dip a bucket in a well and draw it up, whatever is down in that well is what will come out. If bad words are in deep down in me, bad words are going to come out." So she told to me watch what I let into my heart.

As I look back, I still rejoice over the beautiful, edifying words that I heard day in and day out when I was with the Nesters. I was very blessed. At the same time, I am saddened by the many friends who have been destroyed by the weapon of words. I am grieved for the marriages I have seen break apart because words were used the wrong way. I have met countless people whose life dreams and goals were ruined since they were kids, because of the words they heard from family and friends. Poor choices of words have divided and ruined churches, too. *"Death and life are in the power of the tongue, and those who love it will eat its fruits" (Proverbs 18:21).*

The Nesters didn't come up with this by themselves. As believers in Christ, we are called to use our words to edify others. *"Let no corrupting talk come out of your mouths, but only such as is good for building up, as fits the occasion, that it may give grace to those who hear. (Ephesians 4:29).* If we use the weapon of words properly, we might be able to save our relationships, heal broken hearts, build dreams for our young ones, and give hope to the hopeless.

CHAPTER 19

GOD'S PURPOSE IN OUR RELATIONSHIPS

I have spent a lot of time in the previous chapters talking about my relationship with the Nesters, and everything I learnt from it. However the ultimate lesson was that God has a special purpose for in our relationships. God created everything and all of it was good, but He thought it would not be good for man to be alone. Adam did not go to God and say, "I need someone to relate to." God started the relationship between Adam and Eve. Throughout the Old and New Testament, the Bible talks about relationships between different people. God ordained these relationships for a purpose. Consider the relationships of Elijah and Elisha or Timothy and Paul. God had a purpose in bringing the Nesters into my life, purpose that went beyond me getting food, tuition and shelter. God's purpose was for me, through the Nesters, to see His love for me and to draw close to Him.

Like I have mentioned already, I had my struggles as a new believer. In any other relationship, they would have worked against me. However, despite my struggles and weaknesses, the Nesters were there to love and care for me. I remember Mom telling me, on a couple of occasions, "There is nothing you will ever do to make us stop loving you." My earthly adopted parents were telling me this, but their love pointed to God's much deeper love for me.

I seriously started thinking that the only reason God brings people into our lives who love us regardless of our struggles is to give us a taste of His unconditional love and remind us of how much more He loves us. "*If you then, who are evil, know how to give good gifts to your children, how much more will your Father who is in heaven give good things to those who ask him! (Matthew 7:11).* Terry loved me, but he was not dragged from judgment hall to judgment hall for me, he was not falsely accused and flogged in public for me. Above all, Terry did not die a very shameful and painful death on the cross for me.

I thought the Nester's love for me was great, but it pointed to God's love that was greater. I thought their love for me was deep, but it echoed God's love that was deeper. *"No, in all these things we are more than conquerors through him who loved us. For I am sure that neither death nor life, nor angels nor rulers, nor things present nor things to come, nor powers, nor height nor depth, nor anything else in all creation, will be able to separate us from the love of God in Christ Jesus our Lord" (Romans 8:37-39).*

God had a purpose in letting me be loved by the Nesters, but I could not see His purpose clearly. I was focused on the relationship and what it brought me instead of the real reason for the relationship. For a long time, I missed out on a lot of that God had for me in my relationship with the Nesters. I often missed out on opportunities to impact them or let them impact me for God. Terry always told me that everyone needs a relationship like Paul and Timothy had. The Nesters were my Paul, and I was their Timothy and together we had a God -given role to play in each other's lives.

When I fixed my eyes on the relationship instead of the purpose, I found myself striving to draw closer to the Nesters instead of drawing closer to God. My relationship with the Nesters became so important to me that it consumed more and more of my focus. I never wanted to lose their love. I feared talking to Terry about my weaknesses, because I thought, if Terry saw my weak side, he would not love anymore. My reasoning told me that the right thing was to talk to him and let him disciple me and help me through my struggles. However my desire to maintain a good relationship overpowered my reasoning.

This is the time when I struggled more with sin in my life, but I tried so hard to look good before the Nesters because I wanted their approval. I wanted to keep our relationship. Numerous times I lied to Terry and Debbie, just to cover up my sins and look good before them. It was very sad that I was willing to sin against God, who gave me the Nesters, just to keep them.

I have seen others fall into the same trap. We have loved ones that we hold so dear, and we are willing to do whatever we have to do to keep them, even if it means compromising our faith in God. If we have to lie to keep them, then we do exactly that. I have heard of Christians sleeping with their boyfriend or girlfriend because they think sex will help maintain the relationship.

For a while, it felt like I took God off the throne in my life and put the Nesters there. As I watch and listen to some preachers out there, I can't help but think that they have put people, instead of God, on the throne. Their ministries no longer depend on the Most High God, but on the people. They want so badly to keep these people, even if it's at the expense of God. I have listened to some sermons, and I have wondered whether the preacher was trying to please God or the people at his church.

I believe that the main purpose for relationships is that we can help each other draw closer to God. The Nesters were in my life to draw me closer to God. Terry was a friend God brought along to help me on this journey. I struggled, and I was weak, but I was reminded that Christ came to seek and save the lost like me. So I had no reason to put on a mask and hide my brokenness. Terry was my spiritual doctor, and hiding a disease from the doctor only hurts the patient. My relationship with the Nesters was designed to have me focus on my relationship with my Father in heaven, and not so much the Nesters.

I believe the same is true for churches. God does not bring people to church simply so that they can keep attending that particular church and giving tithes and offerings. It is not about making the preachers happy. The main purpose, through church services and fellowship, is to draw these people closer to God.

Relationships are extremely important to us, but the enemy can use the same relationships to turn us away from God and locked in bondage. The main reason I was stuck in Islam was all the relationships that I had within my Muslim community. I became a believer, and the enemy still used relationships to turn me away from God. I remember people telling me how good I had it at the Nesters. Unlike many Ugandans, I had a beautiful house to live in, and I was assured of meals everyday (including a midnight snack). I was loved, my school fees were fully paid, when I got sick I received quality medical help, and more. This all got to my head, so I tried in my powers to keep the relationship. However, I was stupid enough to forget that it was not through my powers that I got the Nesters; it was all the doing of God.

God's purpose was not so much that my relationship with the Nesters would be spotless but that we would help each other grow closer to God. I was talking to Terry one time, and I told him, "You and the Vias have loved me so much that no words will ever express how grateful I am for you." So I asked him what I could ever do to repay him for all he had done and continued doing for me. Terry said, "Keep loving God." That was all. Terry reminded me that it was not about our relationship, but all about God. This relieved me from walking around burdened trying to make the Nesters happy, and trying to make the relationship work. I decided to dedicate my life again to God, and trust Him, who started the relationship, to make it work.

This opened up a door for me to talk to Terry more about my weakness and to let him help me through it. I spent more time learning and letting Terry lead me closer to Christ rather than worrying about the relationship. During this time, I started to make tremendous growth in my faith and develop more as a responsible young man. After this period, the next time I spoke at a youth conference, Terry told me, with tears in his eyes, that he was very proud of me. Later someone asked if I had graduated from seminary, but I pointed to the Paul in my life (Pastor Terry), who took the time to invest in me and groom me to be the young man I was becoming. If I am doing a good job in the pulpit, it's not because I am smart, but because Pastor Terry did a great job as my shepherd. In the end, I hope my Father in Heaven will say, "Well-done. You reached the purpose I set for you in meeting the Nesters."

CHAPTER 20

DAYSTAR UNIVERSITY KENYA

I decided to leave my current school, Jinja, because I wanted to focus more on school. Jinja was in the town, and there were too many distractions. A lot of people knew me, and all this was affecting my education. So I opted for a boarding school away from town. I enrolled at Seroma High School to finish up my A-level (senior year of high school). At the time, Seroma was the biggest Christian school, and I wanted to be in such an environment. Since it was a boarding school, I was not able to see the Nesters as much as I wanted to. Every now and then, though, they did visit me at school.

One significant thing happened while I was at Seroma. The Nesters were back in America on furlough, and I had a vacation. I had to leave school and go somewhere, so I left school to go see my mother. It seems, when some people who hated me saw me, they made a plan to get rid of me. Later that night, "news" went around that I was killed in a car accident. Some missionary friends also were threatened for turning me into an infidel. I did not have a phone so people were calling from America to find out if this was true. It was not, of course, but I had a lot of reasons to be worried. The safest place to be was in school so I went back to Seroma, but the news had already spread there, too. As I walked in, students were very surprised to see me. From then on, they nicknamed me "The Risen Emma" and "The Walking Dead."

I really wanted to go away to somewhere safe, where I could do ministry without having to look over my shoulder all the time. So I decided that, after high school, I would go to university in another country. I graduated from high school, with good grades, and I started looking for universities outside Uganda. I found a good Christian school in Kenya, called Daystar University. I started the application process and, thank God, not too long after, I was accepted. I was excited about the admission but I was scared; this was going to be my first time living in another country.

Time went by quickly. On my last weekend in Uganda, we invited friends to celebrate with me, as I went off to university. Early the next Monday morning, Terry, Natalie and I departed for Nairobi, Kenya. Jonah and Mom had to stay home, I embraced them and kissed them goodbye that morning and the rest of us took off to Kenya. We enjoyed the long journey; we told jokes, laughed, took lots of pictures, and talked about the good times we had had together. Terry kept telling me he could not believe how much I had grown. It was a miracle to me, too, because I was the first in my family to go to university. I remembered that, at one time, I was not even sure I would finish high school. Now I was on my way to university, and my expenses were already paid. God is awesome.

About ten hours later, we arrived in Nairobi. Our first stop was at a store called Nakumatt, where we ate some incredible Mexican food. Then we went to a Nazarene guest house where we stayed for two nights. We had arrived two days before orientation, so we could spend the two days together as a family, before we separated. I wished time would have frozen so that those two days would last forever. I was not sure I wanted to say goodbye. The guest house was beautiful, and Nairobi was way better than my little village back in Uganda. Everything felt different.

In spite of my wish, the two days soon passed, and after breakfast we drove to Daystar University's Athi River campus. This was the day I would check into the dorms and say goodbye to Terry and Natalie. After I put my luggage in my room and I was settled in, Terry and Natalie had to drive back to Uganda. We embraced each other, I cried a lot, they got in the car, and I kept waving as I watched my dad and sister drive away.

Some Kenyan boys passed and saw me crying. I guess they were shocked to see a man cry, or maybe they just thought I was a girl dressed like a boy.

I was used to the life I had with the Nesters. They're the people who understood me best, and loved me most. With them, I had the best life I could have asked for, and now I was alone in the middle of nowhere in Kenya. I started with a bad impression as the crying boy. It didn't look good; I had no idea how life was going to be in Kenya. One thing Dad told me, as I was getting ready for school, was "You are ready, son. Go live for Christ out there." And while everyone was telling me how to survive in Kenya, Mom only said, "Never forget Mama loves so much and she is proud of you." Debbie Nester is such a blessing in my life. She knew exactly what I needed. All I really remembered, throughout the entire semester, was Mama loves me, and she was so proud of me.

The seeds of love that were sown in me at the Nesters were to be tested during this time I was away from them. Was I still going to love God and people, even when the Nesters were miles away? Would university change me? Would I forget the things I learnt from them? These are the questions I pondered during my first week at school. But it was a very difficult first week. I wanted to be home. I kept texting home, until Terry told me to try hard to focus on school and fitting in as a student.

A month went by and I was doing alright. I was not very close to anyone, though, because I still had trouble making friends. In that first month, there were landslides in the Southern part of the country. Daystar University collected clothes and food to send to the people affected by the landslides. Most of the students who signed up to reach out to landslides survivors were sophomores or seniors; I was the only freshman. We went with the supplies we collected and were greeted by many local people, including the leaders. The landslides were so bad that they took lives, destroyed homes, and displaced hundreds of people. When I saw these people, I felt so much compassion for them. I asked the leader of our team if I could share a precious gift with these people.

I was given permission, so I got up to speak. I told the people that all the gifts we gave them were going to be useless if we never shared about the gift of salvation, because ultimately that was the only gift that really mattered. I had with me a really nice, brand new shirt that Natalie bought for me. I took it out and told them that that shirt was precious to me. It was brand new and I had not put it on yet. I called one of the boys and held it out to him. I told everybody that this precious shirt was not going to be his gift until he actually accepted it. I told them that it was the same with the gift of salvation. God is holding it out to us, and we need to accept it, if we are going to have that gift. I explained what the gift of salvation was and why we needed to have it. In the end, a local leader and about three hundred people in that village received Jesus Christ as their Lord and Savior.

We had one more stop to make before going back to school. The leader of the team asked if I could share about salvation at that stop. Of course, I was not going to turn down this opportunity. When we arrived, there were even more people than at the first stop. When our bus pulled up, loads of people gathered around us. The team leader introduced us and explained why we had come. However, before we presented all the gifts, he introduced me to share about Christ first. After I spoke, over two hundred people gave their lives to Christ. After this trip I enjoyed my life in Kenya. I felt like God was already using me and keeping me focused on His ministry.

Since it was an international school, Daystar University had students from all over Africa, some from America and a couple of students from Korea. In Africa, often foreigners from developed countries are viewed as rich people, and many people befriend them for the benefits they could get. I was used to being around foreigners, and I no longer saw them at them as walking banks, but as people who can be great friends. I also learnt from the Nesters that the love or friendship anyone offers is worth more than money or other material stuff.

When I moved to Daystar University, I just wanted to have a friend regardless of whether they were American, Korean or Sudanese. They were going to be my friend because I love them as a friend, not based on what they could do for me. I took some time looking for a friend; I wanted God to bring a friend in my life who was not very different from the Nesters. One day I saw a Korean student on campus. At that time, I did not know much about Korea or Koreans. To me, anyone who looked Asian was probably Chinese and super good at Kung Fu. This was due to my ignorance and watching so many Jackie Chan and Bruce Lee movies. In my mind I started calling him Kung Fu master.

I kept seeing this Kung Fu master on campus, but we never really got to talk that much. He always had people around him, many of whom wanted something or were curious about this man who was very different from the rest of us. Eventually, an opportunity came and we got to hang out. I found out that he was not Chinese. As a matter of fact, it made him upset to be called Chinese. He told me his Korean name, and I immediately forgot it. He asked me what his name was about two minutes later, and I had no idea, so we decided I would call him S, the first letter of his name. I watched a movie that had an Asian man called "Nakamora." It was so easy to memorize this name, so I started calling S Nakamora. He did not like this name, either. He said this was a Japanese name; once more he strongly reminded me that he was not Chinese or Japanese but KOREAN.

The first few days did not go well because I was ignorant about Korea, but S thought I was really funny and somehow different from many other students at Daystar. We found ourselves hanging out more and more. I thought he was a funny little man; the only problem was we could not communicate well because of his English. He had come from Korea to Kenya mainly to take the English classes as an exchange student. Still, we became pretty close friends, and he asked me to be roommates with him. I went to the dormitory office and arranged to leave the room I was staying in, and we became roommates.

S understood my English a lot better than he understood many of the African students, because I did not have a thick African accent. Most of my accent eroded away during my time with the Nesters. This made it a lot easier to communicate with S. I spend time helping him improve his English. S had a funny, but good method of learning English. He watched movies. What made it a funny idea was the specific movie he chose to watch … The Lion King!! The crazier part was that, after we became roommates, I had to watch it with him often to help him with the English. That seemed like a crazy idea, at first, because grown men watching The The Lion King over and over again made no sense. We only watched it in our room, and no one else knew about it because I figured people would laugh at us. Most people were into shows like Prison Break, but we were glued to the computer watching The Lion King.

At first it seemed like it was going to be hard, but sometimes standing through those hard times is what makes a relationship good. So I watched The Lion King with S, and somehow it became fun. It became a good bonding time for us just like I had bonded with Jonah over midnight snacks. We memorized almost all the lines, and we would take turns reciting them. He would be Pumba and I would be Timon, and we would sing the songs from the movie. Listening to him sing these songs with his Korean accent was priceless, and since both of us could not sing to save our lives, it was just too funny. We would see campus couples and break out with "I can see what's happening, and they don't have a clue, they will fall in love and here is the bottom line, our trio is down to two." If you have watched The Lion King, you catch my drift. S and I became very close friends. I missed my brother Jonah a lot, but somehow S was filling that gap up. I started teaching S how to be cool, how to speak cool, based on what Jonah taught me. This was hilarious to witness, as he often changed his voice to sound cool. And the looks on his face whenever he had to be cool; he looked like he needed to be in the bathroom.

With S came a female student from South Korea. Her name was Sophie. S really liked Sophie, and we spent a lot of time talking about Sophie. Unfortunately Sophie was not interested in S as more than a friend. As a way to encourage my man S, I would tell him Sophie was not all that and that he was too good for her. S started to teach me some Korean; he always thought it was funny how I pronounced some words. I didn't know the meaning of the words but later I learnt. S would tell me go and say different things to Sophie, and so I went and said things like, "I love you, Sophie" or "You are my woman, Sophie." He always had fun with this.

I loved this guy as a brother. S was also a believer in Jesus Christ, so we often spent time talking about God and church, he knew how passionate I was for God, and he told me people in Korea love God. He said it would be great for me to visit sometime and do ministry in Korea.

The sad thing, though, was S only attended Daystar University for one semester. When he went back to Korea, it was so hard for us. We had grown so used to seeing each other and having a blast all the time, but that was soon cut short. He told me again that I was welcome to visit him in Korea, and I told him I would pray about that. He made me promise that I would at least try to visit Korea, and when I said I would try, he asked me a few questions. One of the very few things S asked to make sure I was ready to come to Korea was whether I could eat spicy food. I told him eating had never been my problem, and I told him that we had spicy food in Uganda, too. After this he said, "Now you are ready to visit Korea." Little did I know, though, spicy in Uganda does not even come close to spicy in Korea.

The next semester I returned to school, but S had returned to Korea. He had become my best friend and the person with whom I spent most of my time. I felt very empty and burdened with the task of trying to find a new friend like S. There was a new Korean student on campus, and since I had a reputation of being nice to Korean students, he was sent to my room. The recommendation he had received from S was, "Find the Ugandan young man Emma, and your life in Kenya will be a lot better." So this new student did not waste time looking for me, and soon we became roommates.

The new guy was alright but he was nothing like my buddy S. He was taller, he was way too serious about studying, and he barely joked. One time I joked with him the same way I used to joke with S, and he got so angry that I thought he was going to beat me up. However, we tried to make it work. I spent time playing soccer with him, and we both trained on the University team. Like S, this guy did not come alone. He came with a female student, but this time the two actually started liking each other. We barely had any time to hangout because he spent most of it with his girlfriend.

As the semester went on, the harder it became for me to find a friend, and the harder it was for me to enjoy school. About halfway through the semester I received news from my sponsors that they did not have enough funds to take me through university. So, starting with the next semester, they would be no longer financially support me. Most of my financial support came from Rick Via World Reach Ministries, and the Nesters supported me with pocket money. This email came at a time when a time when I was feeling like I did not belong in that university anymore, especially after my friend S left. I knew that God had opened the door for me to get into Daystar University for a reason, and after two semesters, I felt like He was shutting that door. It might sound crazy, but a big part of me believes that the purpose for going to Daystar University was to meet S.

I was bothered by the email from my sponsors, but I was not worried for my own sake. I was more concerned with finding out why they had decided to stop supporting me. I wrote back asking for a reason and expressing my appreciation for all the support they had given me up to that point. Then I turned to God and asked, "Where are you leading me Father?" I was ready to go where God was leading me, because I was certain I was not supposed to stay at Daystar. As the semester came to an end, I told all my friends that I would not be going back to that university. I did not know where I was going to go, but I knew that chapter of my life was coming to a close. I had some fear that, since my supporters had stopped supporting me, I might not return to university at all. However, I found confidence in being still and knowing that God was in control of this all situation.

I left Kenya once the semester ended and returned to Uganda for vacation. I told the Nesters about the email I had received from my supporters in America. But Terry told me not to worry; he said that he would talk to some people about raising support for me to go back to Daystar. I wanted to tell him Daystar was no longer in my plans, but I did not know how to say it without sounding lazy and like I hated school. In Uganda, not many people have the opportunity even to go as far as high school, but I was in university. Money was not a problem, because Terry was willing to raise support for me to go continue studying. If I told him I thought God did not want me to go to Daystar, it seemed it would sound very bad. I had a great opportunity and it would sound like I was throwing it away. Fellow Ugandans would have thought that I was definitely stupid.

Before long, Terry was already talking to people about my school needs, and some people were willing to start supporting me. I decided to finally tell him to stop; I prayed about it and talked to him. I told Terry that I did not want to go back to Daystar University, because I did not feel like God was leading me to go back.

"Well, where is God leading you?" Terry asked. "What is your plan?"

To his disappointment I told him that, while I knew God had a plan, I did not know what it was. Terry loved me like a son, and this is not what he wanted to hear. I sounded very irresponsible to him. It seemed like I was choosing to turn down school without knowing what I was going to do. This seemed like a perfect setup for future failure.

I knew for a fact that I was following the will of God. The only problem was that God did not give me a detailed, four year plan about His will. All I knew was that I was not going to back to Daystar, and even though I had no idea where or why, I knew I was going to go somewhere else. This did not make sense to my family, but sometimes God's call for us might not make sense to our families and friends. Imagine if Abraham had told Sarah, "Honey, you know that boy we waited seventy five years to have? Well God, who gave him to us, is asking me to sacrifice the boy as a burnt offering. So, say 'goodbye' to the boy because he won't be coming back." Sarah easily could have thought Abraham was going crazy in his old age, because this made zero sense. But this was God's call to Abraham. I have learnt that we cannot wait around for people to approve what God is calling us to do. If we do, we are definitely going to miss out on doing the will of our Father in Heaven.

My decision did not make sense to my family, so Terry and Debbie, and others who really cared about me, decided to have a big talk with me. They began by saying, "We love and care about you, and we want to make sure you make the right choices." They also explained that they had had this same talk with their elder son, Daniel, in America. They told me that I needed to be in school or working. Because I was not a boy anymore, I had to start thinking like a grownup. I could not depend on them for too long. All they wanted was for me to seriously consider my future. I had seriously considered my future. I knew who held my future, and the best decision I could ever make for my future was to follow Him who holds my future. That is what I was doing, following the directions of my Heavenly Father. So I held onto my decision of not returning to Daystar.

I decided to pray and seek God's face for more details because I needed my family on my team. As I prayed, I felt like God was leading me to go where my friend S was in South Korea. This sounded crazy to me too, but somehow I had to explain to my family that this is why I decided to quit Daystar. I was to go to South Korea, a place I knew nothing about, a place that spoke a different language, and a place in which I only knew one person. I wanted to follow God; well, He was telling me to go to South Korea. I shared this with my family, but their response was rather negative. I was not sure about anything in South Korea, but if I went back to Daystar, I was sure to have expenses covered. It made no sense that I chose the option which was less certain over going back to Daystar and continuing life as usual. The other people with whom I discussed this issue basically told me not to bother trying to go to South Korea. They told me, if I wanted to go abroad, America was my best option because I already knew so many people there. A move to America made better sense.

I talked to about ten people concerning my desired moved to Korea, and all ten of them advised me not to go. This made me doubt whether the voice I was hearing was really God's voice or just my love for my friend S. I doubted whether God was really leading me to leave Daystar and go to South Korea. Did He really want me to turn down university and go to a place where I did not know if I would be able to ever join school again? The only person that shared the same vision with me about going to South Korea was my friend S. So I did not give up. I started asking God to prepare me for South Korea.

I do not like American Football much, but from having so many American friends, I have grown into the habit of watching the game. In the game there are players, fans and umpires. One peculiar thing about this, and other sports, is that the players play for the umpire and not for the fans. The umpire sets the rules of the game, and the players strive to reach the standards set by the umpire. The first time I watched a Super Bowl game, the Pittsburg Steelers won. What caught my eye the most was the winning play. The player was very close to the line when received the ball. As he landed he tried so hard to keep his toes inside line, and it almost seemed like he was ballet dancing, but he had to do whatever he needed to do to stay inbounds. According to the rules set by the umpire, it was only a touchdown if he stayed inbounds. After he landed, he glanced quickly at the umpire, and the umpire signaled a touchdown. The opposite crowds booed, and yelled at the umpire, but the decision was final. And it was what really mattered.

As believers, God has called us to run this race of faith only according to His rules or standards. We run this race, not for the fans or our families, but for God. Yes, sometimes God might call us to do things that will make our crowds boo, yell or oppose us, but we cannot be bothered by them as long as we can take look at God and see Him saying "touchdown," "thumbs up," "well-done" or "keep going." When the player scores, they do not look to the crowds to determine whether or not it counts, but they look to the umpire. On this journey, God is my umpire. Like that football player, I had to play to please my umpire. If what pleased Him was me going to Korea, I needed to move to Korea.

Another important thing about sports is that the fans are at the game, but they are not in the game. It is very easy for fans to groan and complain, but this is only because they are mere spectators. If you look at my call to move to Korea in terms of sports, God, S, and I were in the game but the rest were simply spectators. They did not know the details of the game, and maybe that is why many were so quick to say not go to Korea. All I really needed were the people who were in the game with me, and they gave me thumbs up to go to Korea. Sometimes people will tell us to not do something, not because they are right, but because they are not in the game do not understand. I made up my mind, so I stopped simply thinking about going to Korea, and I started working hard to make it possible.

CHAPTER 21

JOURNEY TO KOREA

It had been about a year since S told me to try and visit Korea, and I told him I would seek God about it. That is how long it took for God to make me ready to go to Korea. The time was ripe, and I needed to get started on my journey to Korea, the land about which I knew nothing.

I followed Mom and Dad's advice. Since I was not going to school, I needed to work and be responsible, so I worked as a salesman at a small gift shop. I also moved out of the Nesters home and rented a small room on my own. That was the first time I became independent from my family, but I never felt safe outside the Nester's fence. I felt very exposed living on my own. The time that I would have usually spent at the Nester's house playing basketball or just having family time, I spent on the streets looking for something to do. That is when I ran into people who knew me, people who threatened me, and hated me for being a Christian.

Even with all this, I was very confident that it was not going to last for long. I knew that I would soon be on the journey to Korea. I wish it was just as easy as it sounds, but it was not. I still had to apply for the visa, buy a plane ticket, and have the boldness to get on that scare bird (airplane). I looked online and found all the paperwork that I needed for the visa application. The problem was no one helped me with any of the paper work, because no one around me even thought that I should go to Korea. I had to look to God as my sole helper, because I had zero experience applying for a visa.

I was wrong to think I needed all these people to get me to Korea. God did not need anyone in order to do His will in my life. He is God all by Himself. He was calling me to do my part and fully rely on Him to make my journey to Korea possible. So I sent the paperwork to the Korean consulate in Kenya, because we did not have one in Uganda. As I was applying, the people I talked to told me that it would be extremely hard for me to get a visa; for a poor Ugandan like me getting any visa was very rare. To them, my chance of getting a visa on my own was 1%. To me, I had a 100% chance, not because of anything I could do, but because the Great I AM was on my side, and that was all I needed.

The Korean Consulate in Kenya said I needed more paperwork, so I got what they asked for. S sent an email, and now we had to wait and see what the Korean Consulate would say. About four days later, I had a visa to go to South Korea. I did not have a lot of money or influential people helping me, but I had God who worked out everything for me. God did this to show me that He was all I needed. If anyone asked how in the world I got the Korean visa, I would not waste my breathe trying to explain, but give glory to God who got me the visa. My passport came back through DHL; I opened it and there was a stamp in my passport that allowed me to enter Korea. I was not dreaming this was reality. I sat in my little room and worshipped God as I cried.

I told S that I had gotten the visa, and we were both very excited. He started telling me how crazy he would be at the airport. S told me that he was going to cry at the airport when he came to pick me up. I got the visa without a problem. Now I was wondering how I was going to get money for the plane ticket. I did not lose sleep over this issue, because I could trust the same God who gave me the visa to provide money for the plane ticket. The next morning I talked to an older lady, who had actually opposed my idea of going to Korea, who wished to remain anonymous. This lady sold her piece of land, on short notice and for a cheaper price, to buy me a ticket to Korea. So by the end of the day, I had enough money to buy a one way ticket to South Korea.

I went to the Nesters to update them about what was happening and to remind them that this was what God wanted. Terry asked me whether everything was done. All I needed was to book the ticket and get on the plane bound for Seoul Korea, and I told him that God did everything. I gave Terry the money from the older lady, and he used his card to buy me a ticket online. Previously, I had told some people that maybe the only reason I went to Daystar was to open up a door for me to go to Korea. Finally, I got the blessing of my whole family; they understood this was the will of God. The time at Daystar was not a total waste.

I reassured my family that I would try my best to get back into school and study, when I got the opportunity. The decision to leave Daystar was not because I was tired of going to school. I love to be in school, but I placed following God far above school. I held up my end of the promise; by the time you read this, I will have graduated from Myongji University in Seoul, Korea. The Bible says, *"And we know that for those who love God all things work together for good, for those who are called according to his purpose" (Romans 8:28).* Sometimes things happen to us, and they might seem bad and for our hurt, but in the end they work out for good. When I read the email that financial support for school would be cut, I thought this was bad news. However, God used this opened my eyes to think outside the box, and He turned it around to be a blessing in the end.

I prepared for my trip to Korea. I was scared, excited, nervous, happy, and many more emotions all combined. The day came when I was supposed to take flight. I spent my last few hours with my family. It was a precious time of embracing, kissing, crying, praying and saying goodbye. Dad was the last one to embrace me, and he reminded me that he loved me. He told me to stand with God's word, because if I stood with God's word, God would stand with me, and that was all I needed. After that, I took off from Jinja to Entebbe International Airport.

Driving away I was in tears, because I had to leave the Nesters behind. The only thing that comforted me was that I was in the perfect will of God. God brings people into our lives, for a reason and a season. Some stay a short time and some stay for longer. It is a beautiful thing when God puts people in our lives; I enjoyed the people He brought into mine. However, another lesson that I needed to learn was to let go of those people and move whenever God asked me to move. Everyone comes to that point, where we need to let some people go. Yes, sometimes the very things with which God has blessed us are the things He calls us to let go of as we press on for new things that He has in store for us. The only regretful thing would be if we were not good stewards with all God brought into our lives. If we were, we can always look back at the beautiful memories we created with those people, the smiles and good times we had. We can reflect on the good ways we used what God gave us to bring Him glory.

Sometimes God has to take you away from your society, your families and that which is familiar to you so He can bless you from a strange or foreign land. Then, He can do His work in your life without the interruption of your people and environment. And sometimes He moves you away from your people so that he can do a work in you, using some other people. This is not to say that the first people are irrelevant, or did something wrong, ineffective or useless. It is just that their season in your life is over, and it is time for others to invest in you as God leads. I knew that, in taking the next step at that moment, I had to do the hard thing of saying goodbye to my country and to the Nesters. That did not mean that I no longer loved them, but that it was time for me to go share the gift they gave me with the world. Or perhaps there were more gifts God was going to give me through other people in Korea, and I had to obey.

In the Old Testament, God called Abram to leave behind everything he knew. He had to leave his friends and his environment. Many times, leaving can involve losses but it often leads to growth. Look at what happened to Abram. He obeyed and followed God, though God was not very specific with directions, and God blessed Abram. He changed his name to Abraham, the father of all nations; it was through Abraham that God made the promises to deliver the Israelites. Abram was one thing at his home with his friends and in his environment, but he was a better person after he decided to follow God's leading. One thing that might be standing in our way to spiritual growth is the fact that we are not willing to separate from certain habits, people, behaviors or environments.

In 2 Kings 2, Elisha had to let Elijah go. Elisha was a servant, a helper, a student and a minister to Elijah. These two were close, and I imagine, if it were up to Elisha, he would have rather had Elijah around all the time. But God was getting ready to do something new in Elisha's life. Elijah's work in Elisha's life was finished. So God was going to take Elijah away from Elisha, therefore Elisha had to let Elijah go. But it was after the separation that Elisha received a double portion of the blessings that Elijah had.

I know it is very hard. We form relationships, and sometimes we are unwilling to let those people go. It should almost make sense that God brings people in our lives for a purpose, and when that purpose is completed, they go. Jesus had a purpose here on earth. He surrounded Himself with twelve men that He loved dearly, but when His purpose was fulfilled he had to go. The disciples went on to do great things after the separation; they healed the sick, gave sight to the blind and turned the world upside down for Christ. The most comforting thing is that, if these people are believers in Christ, we really never say "goodbye." It's only "see you later." The separation is only temporary.

We have friends, family and all sorts of people in our lives. Like Abraham, sometimes we will have to choose between keeping company with these special people and moving on to God's call for us. Dedication often requires separation; it is hard for the two to move together. Jesus' dedication to God often required His departure from the crowds and from his own disciples. The same was true with Abraham. When God separates us, He often blesses us with new ministries. Paul was separated from his friends in prison, but it was in prison that he wrote many of his Epistles. If we are going to obey the great command to go and make disciples of all nations, we should embrace separation. It may be a departure from people, a location, or certain activities. For example, the twelve disciples had to leave behind their fishnets and other occupations.

This is easy to say but hard to do; one of my biggest and fears in life is separation from the people I love. I have lost so many people along the way that now I want to hold on to everyone who comes into my life. But in those struggles to let go, we ought to listen to God telling us that serving

Him is more important than keeping relationships. We also can trust the same God, who brought our loved ones into our lives, to bring new people. God has blessed us all with a unique gift, and He calls us to share with the world. However, if we are stuck holding onto people and things, we will not be so effective sharing that gift with the world.

I have watched many people cause themselves great pain by holding on when God is saying let go. Sometime we must stop trying to fix the relationship, stop fighting to keep the job, and break that habit. The enemy keeps us bound and inactive by convincing us that we cannot survive without these things. But I have learnt that the only thing which we cannot do without is Jesus Christ. God is calling us from these prisons where we have been trapped. In order to follow God's calling, I had to let go of everything I knew in Africa. That is why I was on the way to Entebbe International Airport.

I arrived at the airport and passed through all the check points. There is a place in the airport where, once you pass through, the person who escorted you is left behind. All they can do is wave. I found that place when I passed through Immigrations, and it hit me. *This was really happening.* From this point forward everything was new to me. I had never flown before, and now I felt like I was walking with my eyes closed. However, I had to let God walk me through the darkness. Korea was a foreign land to me, and I knew only one person there. I really had to depend on God to guide me.

We boarded the plane. I had a window seat because I wanted to look out and wave goodbye to my country as the plane took off. However, the takeoff was scary. I felt like throwing up. Thank God, that didn't happen … for my sake and for the sake of the big man sitting next to me. The plane ascended into the clouds, and my country grew smaller until it disappeared. Right at that moment, when I could not see my little country anymore, I told God to take full control. This plane was not direct to Seoul. I had two layovers in Ethiopia and Hong Kong before arriving in Korea. A few hours later, the plane landed in Ethiopia. Two hours later, I got on the plane for Hong Kong. The flight to Hong Kong was longer, about eight hours long. The airport in Hong Kong was a lot nicer than those in Uganda and Ethiopia. There were also a lot more international people.

In Hong Kong, something very scary happened. Since I was switching from Ethiopian Airlines to Cathay Pacific, I needed a new boarding pass for the next flight. At the ticket counter, the lady asked for my documents, but as she read through my documents, she had a strange look on her face. I asked her, "Ma'am, is there a problem?"

"There is a big problem," she said. "According to the Korea immigration rules, with your tourist visa, you must have a return ticket booked." But remember I only had enough money to buy a one way ticket to Korea. And I had no idea about these rules. So she told me that, unless I bought a return ticket on the spot, she would not be able to issue me a boarding pass. I had only about $300 USD, and it for living expenses my first few weeks in Korea. Buying a new ticket on the spot was not an option. I was in a foreign land with no friends, nothing familiar, and not enough money. But I had God.

Walking with your eyes closed is difficult, because you have to rely on the person hold your hand. I was trusting God to keep directing me. Sometimes God puts us in situations where our money, our friends, and even our self cannot help the situation. Only God can help, so that in the end, only God receives the glory.

At the ticket counter, I asked the lady to excuse me for a few minutes while I went to talk to someone. I walked around the airport and found I quiet spot, and I went to God in prayer. I was not in control; only God was, so I talked to Him to find a solution. I knew God was leading me to Korea, not Hong Kong, so I wanted to make sure He did not change His mind. As I prayed, in my heart I was given confirmation that I was headed to Korea. This ticket problem was just a storm along the way. This storm was not meant to not to stop me from going to Korea, but to teach me to depend on God.

On that day, when evening had come, he said to them, *"Let us go across to the other side." And leaving the crowd, they took him with them in the boat, just as he was. And other boats were with him. And a great windstorm arose, and the waves were breaking into the boat, so that the boat was already filling. But he was in the stern, asleep on the cushion. And they woke him and said to him, "Teacher, do you not care that we are perishing?" And he awoke and rebuked the wind and said to the sea, "Peace! Be still!" And the wind ceased, and there was a great calm" (Mark 4:35-39).*

When Jesus says we are going to the other side, it means that we are going to the other side. Period. He does not promise us that the ride will always be smooth. When we face storms, they do not change the fact that we will get to the other side. The enemy will attempt to make us quit, but he has no authority to stop us. The only person that has authority is the one who said we are going to the other side. He is the one on whom we need to focus.

God said I was going to Korea. Yes, along the way there were some storms, like the one at the Cathay Pacific ticket counter, but that storm was not going to stop me from getting to my destination. I was a little bit scared, and I understand why the disciples freaked out. Storms are scary, but they are only scary when we focus on the storms. Instead of focusing on how big they, we should be look to the Great I AM. The disciples eventually sought Jesus to calm the storm; I also went to God to calm my storm. In verse 39, Jesus rebuked the wind and the waves, and all was completely calm. We serve a mighty God! However big our storms might be, God is bigger and more powerful, and therefore we can trust Him to calm all our storms.

After praying, I went back to the Cathay counter. The same lady was there, but something was different about her this time. She was calm, and she had my boarding pass ready—the same boarding pass that, a few moments earlier, she was not going to give me. She gave me the boarding pass and told me the gate number for boarding, but she also told me that I might have some trouble when I arrived at aiport in Seoul. God came through for me at this particular moment and calmed my storm in Hong Kong. I didn't have to spend any extra money to buy another ticket, yet I was given my boarding pass to Seoul Korea.

I got on the plane and we headed to Seoul, but I never slept on that flight. I was praying, preparing for the upcoming storm at Incheon International Airport immigration. About four hours later, I found myself in line to go through immigration. When my turn came, the officer seemed to take a long time looking at my documents. He called over another person, who person also looked at my documents. Then I was asked to follow the second gentleman to an office. In that office, we were joined by a third man. He did not smile much, and he looked rather upset. He asked many questions, some about my finances and why I was coming to Korea. Some questions I could not answer. The immigration officers took a short break to discuss amongst themselves.

The room became quiet for a little while and this was my cue to go back to God. I asked Him to calm this storm too. A few minutes later an older gentleman came in, but he was different. He had a smile on his face, he asked me to give him S's phone number. He called S to make sure he was there ready to pick me up. Indeed S had been waiting for me since early morning. This gentleman hung up the phone and said, "You are free to go meet your friend. Enjoy your visit in Korea, but be sure to leave when your time of stay expires."

Many of us are going to go through storms as we seek to follow God. They come in many forms, like relational and financial problems and sickness, but I am here to testify that no storm is too big for God. When we go through storms, we should not look at them but look at God, who is our help. David said,

"I lift up my eyes to the hills. From where does my help come?
My help comes from the LORD, who made heaven and earth.
He will not let your foot be moved; he who keeps you will not slumber.
Behold, he who keeps Israel will neither slumber nor sleep.
The LORD is your keeper; the LORD is your shade on your right hand.
The sun shall not strike you by day, nor the moon by night.
The LORD will keep you from all evil; he will keep your life.
The LORD will keep your going out and your coming in
from this time forth and forevermore" (Psalm 121).

If we do look at our storms, they should cause us to get on our knees and call on the name of Jesus.

Just like that, I was through that storm, and I went to the waiting area to meet my friend S. A lot of people were waiting outside. To my surprise, at that moment I saw at least ten men that looked exactly like S. I ran up to one man, thinking he was S, but he looked at me very strangely. I thought people might think I was crazy and call the police on me if kept approaching people like that.

I still had trouble memorizing S's full name. Maybe I just never tried since I had other names I called him. His full name is Kim Sung Jin, but I only remembered "Kim." I thought I would just go to the information counter and ask if they knew my friend, Kim. But when I asked, someone told me it would take at least two days to find him, because there was probably more than one hundred Kim's there at that moment. That wasn't counting women or kids.

As far as I could see I was the only black man at the airport that morning, so decided to sit in one central place and wait for S to notice me. The problem was he was waiting for me to come out another gate. So he called the office where I had been questioned, and they told him which gate I had used. Eventually, I saw someone running toward me, and as he got closer, he screamed, "Emma, Emma!" Then I knew for sure this was my man S. S embraced me and said, Welcome to my humble home" (we learnt this line from Timon and Pumba in The Lion King). We did our secret hand shake, and we kept saying, "I cannot believe this is happening!" Honestly part of me thought this was a dream. We were both very happy and loud, but we did not care who watched us.

Right outside that gate was a McDonald's. I had seen this restaurant in movies and pictures and Jonah had told me about often. So when S asked where I wanted to eat at, my mind was already made up. You have to remember that Jonah and I had the gift of eating. I get too excited when it comes to food, and now I was super excited to try this famous McDonald's for the very first time. We ordered and sat down, but it seemed like the waitress took forever to bring our meals out. It was only a couple minutes, but it seemed so long to me. I just wanted my burger on the spot. When our food came, I immediately dug in. S stopped me and reminded me that we needed to pray first. I was so excited about the food, that prayer was the last thing on my mind. We prayed and I devoured that burger. It didn't last long, but it tasted very good.

I felt like I had missed out on the good food for a long time after trying a MacDonald burger. I wasted twenty one year's eating healthy Ugandan. I had compared my journey to Abraham's journey, but I am sure I had a much better treat; I bet Abraham would have wanted to run into a MacDonald, too. Before coming to Korea, many friends told me that people in China eat very strange things like snakes, frogs, dogs, monkeys, cat and strange sea animals. In Uganda, no one made a difference between China and Korea. All of Asia was called China. As a person who loves to eat, this was a big concern for me, because I was not sure whether I would like eating snakes. Maybe God was going to give me a new appetite so monkeys and dogs would taste like chicken.

At McDonald's, though, all my concerns were put to bed. I was very comforted to know that the first food I ate in Korea was not a cobra. I had listened to ignorant people who had never been to Korea, to think I was going to eat such food. I thought to myself that, if I did encounter strange food, I could always go back to McDonald's for a Big Mac. As a matter of fact, I was ready to have one diet for my entire time in Korea: McDonald's. After five years in Korea, though, I do not like McDonald's anymore. I have found better burgers and better Korean food.

After McDonald's, we bought tickets to Busan, S's hometown, which is about four hours away from Seoul. Moments later, we departed for Busan. The bus was very nice, very comfortable and even air conditioned. I took a window seat because I wanted to see what Korea looked like as we traveled. It was a habit of mine to always take windows seat and watch because I never slept on buses. The few times I tried I was forced awake because of the horrible roads and potholes in my country. It always felt like you were in some kind of machine that was rigorously shaking you. So I assumed

I would not sleep and just look out the window, but the roads were so smooth, and the seats were very comfortable. After about ten minutes I was sound asleep. I woke up a few times and went right back to sleep. It was awesome.

Four hours later, we arrived at the Busan bus terminal, and again S told me, "Welcome to my humble home." We dragged my luggage out of the terminal to where cabs were waiting. The cab driver was so nice he help us load the luggage into the car, and he seemed very excited to see me. This car was too nice to be a taxi. I had never been in a nicer car than this cab. It was amazing how good things were in Korea. The roads were spotless, the bus was comfortable and air conditioned, the cab was excellent, and don't forget my new favorite place in the world, McDonald's.

CHAPTER 22

DOWN SOUTH / BUSAN

A few moments later the cab pulled up to S's home. His mom was there and she warmly welcomed us. She was speaking to me in Korean, but if I assumed it was all good stuff judging by the big smile on her face. Inside the house was very different from what I was used to in Uganda and Kenya. S's mother fought so hard to say some English words to me, but every single time all that came out was "thank you." I wish I spoke some more Korean, but all I knew in Korean was "Jesus loves you," "Don't leave me" and "How are you?" Especially that first week in Korea, I wish I had learnt the Korean word for constipation, because that was my first big problem from eating too much rice. S had learnt some English in Kenya but I guess when he went back to Korea he stopped using English. He had forgotten a lot of it, so he could not help me as much.

S's mom offered me some drinks, and then she told S to let me take a nap since I was very tired. They did not have a guest room in the house so I was given S's room and S was to sleep in the living room. I took a shower, changed clothes and took a nap. Later S woke me up to have dinner with his mom. She had spent almost all day preparing a good meal for me as a special visitor; she was very appreciative that I looked out for S when he was in Kenya, so she wanted to give me a good treat.

The dinner table was very small, and we had to sit down on the floor as we ate. This was surprising to me because, in Uganda, usually only women and kids sit on the floor while eating. But I was not about to complain. I was now in Korea, not Uganda and I was going to do as the Koreans did. However sitting down and enjoying the meal was a pretty hard task, since my legs went to sleep a couple times. I changed sitting positions repeatedly because I was very uncomfortable.

There was a lot of food on the table in small bowls, but the only thing that looked familiar was white rice, and also tiny fish on another plate. I never really liked fish that much. The only times I ate fish was when Mama Debbie fried tilapia, and usually it was boneless or the bones were big enough to pick out. But I was given this tiny little fish, and the one thing on my mind was how difficult it must be to pick out the bones. As if that was not bad enough, I was handed two little sticks to use for eating the fish. I didn't know what in the world was I supposed to do with these two sticks.

S and his mom where using them just fine. I tried almost every possible way to eat with the sticks: poking, dragging and carrying the food. Everything I tried failed. I thought, if this is how I was going to be eating in Korea, I was going to lose a lot of weight. There was no way in this world that I was going to be able to use these sticks. So I decided to drop the sticks and use my hands like we often did in Uganda. S's mom stopped me and decided to help me. She picked all the bones out of my fish, but I still could not get the fish up from the plate to my mouth. Hard times call for drastic measures; she did something very embarrassing to me. She fed me like one would feed an infant, and the more embarrassing thing was that when she started feeding me, I opened my mouth like an infant to eat. I never said, "No I am an adult. I will feed myself." If this happened while I was in Uganda all my friend would make fun of me so much, and my pride would be destroyed. S just seemed to have fun watching everything that happened, and I dared him to tell stories to anyone about my new feeding experience.

Remember, in Kenya, the only question S asked when I accepted his invitation to visit Korea? He asked whether I could eat spicy food, and I told him I eat everything, so he passed this information on to his mother. She had this notion, that I could eat spicy food, in her mind when she prepared the meal. And she prepared a lot of it because she also heard that I had a big appetite. However, Ugandan spicy was like an infant and Korean spicy was like a ninety year old man. To make matters worse, as we ate, S started telling me about Korean cultures regarding food. He explained that it was not nice to leave food on the table. For one thing, his mom spent all day cooking. Also Korea previously was a poor country with very little to eat, so they just didn't like to waste food. Basically, this meant I had to eat all my food.

After being fed the fish with the chopstick, I reached for other food that I could eat with a spoon. I had no idea what I took, but it looked pleasing to my eyes. I took a bite, and it was out-of-this-world spicy. It was so spicy that, after the first few bites, I literally lost my voice. I started sweating like I had been working out, my eyes turned red, and my lips were on fire. However, I had loaded my plate with a mountain of food, and I was not about to waste it and offend the Korean culture. The crazy thing, though, was that they kept asking whether the food was delicious and the only answer they were looking for was, "Yes, it is very delicious." And through all this I had to remain calm and try to regain my voice to say, "Wow this is a great meal." I could not eat slowly anymore, so I decided to just shove down whatever remained on my plate so I could get be done.

I cleared my plate, and I was thinking, "Thank God, I am still alive after that spicy attack." I sighed with relief, and I wiped the tears out of my eyes. And then S's mom loaded my plate with another serving and she said, "Mani mogo" (which means "eat a lot"). But I knew that the moment I ate any more of that spicy food, I would wake up in the emergency room … or in Heaven. So I told S that the first serving was very delicious, but I was too stuffed to eat anymore.

Moments later S's father and older sister came back home. They worked until late, seemed very tired and did not speak much English, so our greetings were short. It was a Saturday night, and we had to get up early the next morning to go to church so, I said good night to everyone and went to bed. Fortunately, breakfast the next morning was not as spicy as dinner, and there was still rice on the table, so I had something familiar to eat.

On the way to church S explained that he had told a lot of people about me, and the friends in his youth group could not wait to meet me. He had told them that I was a funny guy, but I was also nice and loved God. We got to church a few minutes late, so people were already seated as we walked in. It seemed like all heads turned to face the door. I did not want to be in the spot light, so I sat in the back next to a sleepy old man. However, when the pastor went up to preach he talked about me and S, and then he invited up me to give a greeting. I gave a very short greeting and went back to my seat.

When I sat down, the old, sleepy man did something I thought very strange. He rubbed my thigh with his hand and smiled. I was thinking in my head, "Old man, your hand is about to be broken if you do not keep it to yourself." But later I found out that Korean older people are very touchy especially when they express their affection. Not too long after that, an older woman patted my butt, but this time I knew her motives.

After the church service, I remained behind to hang out with the young people. They had all sorts of questions for me. They were very curious about me. I learned that I was the first African to visit the church.

One of the couples invited me and some other church members to their house for dinner. I wanted to turn this down because of the dinner experience the previous night. However, S accepted the invitation for me, so I had no choice but go. The hosts were a newlywed couple, and they had prepared a variety of foods, especially fruit. Their house was a lot bigger than S's house. The pastor also came to visit, but to my surprise, everyone that walked in just sat on the floor leaving a beautiful couch unattended. I wanted sit there because my legs were killing me from sitting on the floor, but I was a little scared what the people sitting down would say. I learned, though, that it was not wrong to sit in the couch. Koreans were used to sitting on the floor, so they did not mind it, and they didn't mind me sitting in the couch either. That night I ate a lot of fruit and rice. Some fruits, like strawberries, I had never had before. These people welcomed me warmly, more than I expected, and all these good things reflected God's love and care for me even in a foreign land.

We left to go back to S's home, and on the way we made plans about what we were going to do the next day. S told me that a long line of his friends wanted to meet me, because they had heard a lot about me from S. Also Sophie, from Kenya, also wanted to see me. So we decided that we would go out Monday morning after breakfast and spend the entire day meeting people, and at night we would play basketball. As we made plans, I had a specific plan for what I wanted to see as we went out the next morning. I was not going tell S because I feared he would judge me. Before I came to Korea, I was a big fun of Chinese Kung Fu movies. I really enjoyed how they fought. Some of that fighting seemed impossible to Ugandan men, but Chinese people could do it. I watched a lot of Jackie Chan, Bruce Lee and Jet Li movies throughout the years. The same things I saw in Chinese movies, I was sure I would also see on the streets in Korea. Ignorantly, I thought Korean and Chinese were same people in different countries, like Ugandans and Kenyans. So I thought I would walk around town and see at least three people get in an argument and pull out all the Kung Fu moves. More than meeting all S's friends, I was anticipated the fights I was about to witness.

Morning came and one of S's friends picked us up, and we went around meeting people. Of course they were curious and had questions for me, but as we toured the city I was looking out anxiously, waiting to see a fight. Evening came and we went to one of the universities played basketball for a little while. Then went to Haeundae Beach at night, but I still saw no fights. No one walked around in the orange Shaolin temple gowns, either. The closest thing was a few kids in the taekwondo uniforms. I felt disappointed, but I figured that was not a good day. Eventually, I had to learn that real life was very different from the movies. Besides, as a Christian I should not want to see fights like that, so it's a good thing I saw none.

On the way home, S and I stopped somewhere to talk. This Monday was my third day in Korea. S gave me some heart breaking news that he had not shared before I got on the plane to Korea. He said that, by the end of the week, he had to move to Seoul to study and prepare for an exam in order to get a job. The scariest part was that he could not take me with him because the place where he would be staying was a study room only meant for one person. After I heard this news, I lost my energy and had to sit down. Here I was in a foreign land, and the only person I knew was about to leave me. Without S, I could not stay at his home, so somehow I had to get shelter. If I didn't have shelter, that meant I would homeless in Korea, and then I would be required to leave the country.

Have you ever felt like God makes no sense whatsoever? For me this did not make any sense. S was the only person I knew, I needed him around at least to help me settle in or teach me some Korean that would help me get around. His leaving made zero sense. Did I come to Korea to be with my friend, only for him to leave me homeless and helpless, to have to go back to Uganda only after two days? It is times like this when it becomes very hard to tell people God was leading me to Korea. It made no sense at all, and I started doubting whether I was even following the call of God. I imagined the shame I would endure telling my friends back in Uganda that it was not really God's will for me to be in Korea. Maybe, in the same way, it made no sense for a mother who had already lost her husband, to lose her only son in Luke 7. But God shows up to make sense out of what seems to be nonsense to us. For the widow, Jesus brought her son back to life. Jesus turned things around and made perfect sense of them. It didn't make sense that Joseph was sold into slavery and tossed into prison, but God meets us at the point of nonsense and turns things around to make sense.

When I left Uganda I knew that I had to trust God. I had to completely depend on Him. Through the conversation I had with S, though it did not make sense to me at first, I could hear God tell me that He was all I needed. God led me to Korea, but His purpose was not for me to just have a good time with my friend S. God had used S to bring me to Korea, but God did not need S to be around me for Him to bless me and keep me in Korea. Furthermore God was teaching me to trust Him even more. I was starting to place my trust in S, but God was taking S out of the picture so that I would completely rely on Him. Also, when I look back now, I can say it was only because of God that I have made it this far in Korea. It was hard, but I had to go back to being blind and letting God guide me.

After that conversation, I told S that I would pray about things, and S said he would talk to people to see if we could get some help. The next day, Tuesday, a couple more friends wanted to meet me, so we met them and played basketball and soccer. We visited a nearby university, and for some reason people took pictures of me, and wanted to touch my hair. Later, we had plans to help out at a home for the disabled, and as we waited for our ride S and I had time alone to talk. Again we went back to that conversation we had last night because he had gotten some feedback from the people he had talked to, but it was not very good. This time S asked me what my plans were. I guess the people he had talked to all asked him about my plan. I told him that I really had no plan, except follow God and the directions He was giving me.

If I really had a plan to go to a foreign country, it would not have been Korea. I would have been in the UK or USA, but not Korea. In Korea, I was on God's plan not my plans. However, telling S that I had no plan seemed to frustrate him, because people wanted to know my plan before they even thought of helping me. S was maybe frustrated about going back to tell these people that I had no plans. He blamed me for being poor at planning, and somewhat childish. He told me that was not how the world works, because in the real world people must make plans. S was very right that, in the world, we have to make plans. But this was not a business trip or a vacation over which I had power, this was a call to follow God and He was in full control. He made the plans and I followed.

God told Abraham, "*Go … to the land* I will show you" *(Genesis 12:1).* I bet if you asked Abraham where he was going, he would not have told you he was going to Michigan or Italy. I think he would have said, "I am going where God is leading me. God never gave details about the place, but He simply said I will show you the place." This is almost the same as God saying, *"I will let you know as you obey and follow me."* Many times God is really testing our faith and obedience by not laying out everything for us. In Luke, Jesus met ten lepers who cried out to him for healing. Instead of healing them on the spot, Jesus said, "*Go and show yourselves to the priests" (Luke 17:14).* They did not say, "Wait a minute, Jesus; we came for healing, not to be sent on a journey." Even though they were not healed immediately, they obeyed and went to show themselves the priests. So as they went, their healing began. Sometimes all we have to do is obey and go, and God will start to bless us even as we walk. On my journey in Korea, all I had to do was to obey and keep following God, and He would show me the way.

But we live in a business-minded world where planning is demanded. We prefer to walk by sight and not by faith. In a leadership meeting, if you dare say you do not have a plan but are following God's plan, you might just get fired. We want to see plans on paper. That is what S and all of his contacts wanted to see, but I did not have that. However, I told S the one thing I was sure of, that I was going to become a student at a university in Korea. This seemed like a better plan to S, so the next day we drove to his university, Kosin, and we inquired about admission there. This was when S realized that I actually did not have the money to pay for school. They had to give me a full ride scholarship in order for me to be a student, but Kosin was not ready to give me that scholarship.

S was very frustrated, and for a minute the look on his face seemed to *say I made a mistake inviting Emma to Korea when I cannot take care of him.* S was in a predicament. He had to go study in Seoul, but he could not just leave me homeless. Wednesday night S told me that he was already late for Seoul; he had changed the dates because of my visit. If he delayed longer he risked losing the opportunity completely. I understood how S felt, but he never seemed to understand why I was peaceful and not scared about the whole situation. He told me that, if no solution was reached by his departure time on Friday, the best move would be to send me back to Uganda. He said he was very sorry he had let me down. He did not know, though, that I did not have a return ticket to Uganda, and he did not know that I was in Korea on God's directions not his.

I told S that God would make a way out of no way. I told him everything would be okay, and that I trusted God to look out for me. Nevertheless, S had trouble believing that, because most of the people with whom he had talked would not give me a place to stay. All day Thursday went by and we still had no solution. That night we were sitting hopelessly in S's home.

He was thinking of taking me with them to Seoul the next morning and leaving me at the airport. I prayed to God, and asked God to open a door for me. A couple minutes later, S received a phone call from one of his church members who stayed in another area called Cheonan. It was about two hours away from Seoul. They said they would like for me to stay with them for a short time while I figured out what I would do next. S came into the room with a smile on his face and told me to pack my bags. There was a home for me in Cheonan.

This church member attended a Bible school in Cheonan and only returned to Busan over the weekends for worship and to see his family. I reminded S again that God would take care of me, and make a way out of no way. We had just a few hours to reach a major decision and God intervened right on time. But still S had trouble believing. He said the new home was only temporary, and told me I had to work hard to get into school. Even that seemed impossible since I had no money to pay tuition. I told him that, after a few months, I was going to call him to testify of how God was blessing me in a foreign land. S told me that, if that happened, he would never doubt God again.

The next morning we packed and prepared to leave. I could see the sadness on S's mom's face. She knew my pain but had no idea how to help. I hugged her goodbye and she gave me a gift, a towel that I still have, and in English she said "goodbye."

CHAPTER 23

FISH TRUCKS AND NAZARENES

We climbed into a taxi and left for the train station. The train to Cheonan was my first time ever aboard a train. I was holding onto the scripture, *"Let us hold fast the confession of our hope without wavering, for he who promised is faithful" (Hebrews 10:23).* God is faithful and does not lie. If God promised He would never leave me nor forsake me, I could trust Him. If He promised to bless me, I could trust him. If He promised to take care of me, I could trust Him because He is faithful. God's promises were coming true even as we got on the train for Cheonan.

In the very first week in Korea, the enemy was already waging war on me and my calling. But even though the enemy might win some battles, he will never win the main war. It's true that I could not live in Busan any longer, but I never went homeless. And though my friend was going away, I was not going to be alone, because I gained two new friends.

We got off the train after about two hours, and we went to Calvary Chapel. This was the school attended by the gentlemen who had invited me, and they were at school all day. Upon arrival we met some American professors who ran and taught at this school. While talking with the American professors, I asked whether it would be possible for me to join their school so that I could have something to do in Korea. I was thinking this could be a good way to extend my visa once the three months ended. But they had the same concern about fund. Also, since this school was not accredited, they could not help me get a visa. That was a no, but it did not bother me because I knew that God had a school for me that would say "yes." S and I grabbed lunch in the neighborhood. After lunch, S had to say goodbye and continue on to Seoul. It was sad to say goodbye after just about a week with my friend. He told me he was very worried and asked me to call him for anything, but I told him to go and study in peace. I was in good hands—God's hands—and He was going to take care of me the way He saw fit.

My new housemates would leave in the morning for school and came back at night. So I would clean the house and then walk around the neighborhood during the daytime. There was not a lot for me to do. There was a middle school right next to the house and it had a basketball court, so I would go shoot basketball almost every evening. For some reason, perhaps because I was the only black man in the neighborhood, I always attracted a huge crowd of kids and people passing by. I remember walking around the neighborhood one day when an old man walked up to me with a very excited look on his face. He put two thumbs in the air and he screamed "Obama!"

I was taught that one of the things you want to do when you get into a new society is make new friends. Every morning, when I walked out of the house, there was an old man I passed. He was like the apartment care taker. He was always very friendly. He always smiled and said some few things at me in Korean. I figured I could make new friends beginning with this old man, and I expected it to be pretty easy since he was already very friendly. I tried to speak broken English thinking it would translate into Korean. I repeated myself many times and spoke louder, but it never worked. I was simply trying to tell him that we are friends. When the two gentlemen I stayed with came home that night, I asked them for the Korean word for "friend," and I was told "chingu." The next morning I went back and I told the old man that he and I were "chingus," but something very strange happened. I thought that he would smile and agree with me, but instead he seemed upset, and he stopped being friendly to me.

The old man told me how old he was, and I kept saying, "No, chingu. Chingu! Not your age." The old man got upset and asked me to leave. That day went very badly, and I had no idea exactly why. So I went back to the guys I was staying with and asked them what I did wrong in wanting to be friends with someone. They explained that, in Korea, it is very disrespectful that a boy my age would want to be friends with an older person. If I needed friends, I had to find people of my age. However, where I come from, you can be friends with whoever wants to be your friend. It does not matter how old they were especially man to man. I learnt my lesson and stopped trying to make friends with older people.

Usually I went to church every Sunday. My first week in Cheonan I missed church and I didn't like it, so I looked online for a church I to attend in the future. I needed to be a part of a church. I found a couple of English-speaking churches, and I chose to go to the one that was closest to where I was staying. It met in at Korea Nazarene University (KNU International English Church), and the main pastor was Joshua Broward. When I visited for the time, I enjoyed really it and thought it would be a great place to visit again. Also I felt absolutely relieved to see some other foreigners. Even better, I saw an African man at this church. That was a huge relief because I was beginning to think I was the only African in all of Korea. At this church I met a lot of young adults, most of whom were English teachers. I quickly bonded with them on the grounds that we were foreigners living in Korea.

The Tanzanian man at church told me more about Korea from an African man's perspective. He also told me that it would be very important to get cheap phone so that anyone could reach me anytime if they needed me. So I used the little money that I had to get a cheap pay-as-you-go phone.

As I met new people, the question that I was asked most was, "What brings you to Korea?" I always had trouble answering because my answer was never a short sentence like, "I am teaching English" or "I am a student." People also often asked where I was from. When I told them, the next question would be, "Why Korea?" I would just say, "It's a long story." Some people, including Pastor Josh, wanted to hear this long story. I told them I would be glad to tell it whenever they had time. When I said this to Pastor Josh, he replied "Why don't I buy you lunch on Tuesday and we can get to know each other better?"

You are never going to guess where Pastor Josh wanted to have lunch!! McDonald's! I had not even told him how much I loved the place, but he picked it, so this was my second time at McDonald's. However, this time I was more relaxed than I was at the airport. We ate and talked, Pastor Josh welcomed me to his church, and he told me that there was a gentleman from Tanzania serving on the church board. Pastor Josh was very nice. He introduced me to his wife and his little girl, Emma. You heard that right. A little girl named Emma. This is when I learnt that, in Korea, Emma was strictly a girl's name. From that time on, I went by my full name, Emmanuel. I told him Pastor Josh story why I was in Korea and of my desire to get into school. He mentioned that it might be worth trying Korea Nazarene University. He thought that I had a good chance of getting a scholarship there. He promised he would write a good recommendation for me as I kept going to his church.

Pastor Josh talked to more people about me, especially young adults in their twenties. They started hanging out with me, and they welcomed me into their groups. I remember this young man, Wynn Arellano, who played guitar in the church. He used to invite me to group activities. A couple of the expatriates, including Pastor Josh, played soccer at night after work. I was invited to play with them one night. This game was foreigners versus Koreans. I scored two goals in the very first game I played, so they enjoyed having me on the team. That night, I met another special friend. Victor Marquez was one of the nicest people in the world. He was not really a great soccer player but he liked to come out and enjoy the fellowship. Victor and I became very close friends. Eventually he introduced me to his wife Katie, and Katie introduced me to her friend Amy.

KNU became my favorite spot to hang out at during day. I would go spend some time with my new friends there if they were not working, and I also began visiting the admission office to see about admission into the university on a full ride scholarship. They let me use the library at the university, but I did not really study. Instead I used this time to watch the entire Jack Bauer 24 series.

Word was spreading quickly in the university about me, especially among the expats. I was introduced to a professor named Bondy. He had heard a little bit about me, and he wanted to know more. So we set up times that we met and talked. Professor Bondy was about fifty years old, but we became very close friends. He was teaching Christian Education at the university, and he was also a preacher at one of the nearby churches. When he heard my story, he felt like God could use me in the university and in Korea. So Professor Bondy wasted no time filling my schedule. On one night when he was supposed to speak at a nearby church, he gave me half the time to speak with the assistance of a translator.

During some school chapels Professor Bondy had me speak to the students. He held a Bible study at his house, and he let me speak there, too. He would invited me to speak in some of his classes. I felt like his right hand man. The Christian Education department of the school had a big seminar in Seoul, and a lot of students were going to go there. Professor Bondy picked me to be one of the representatives at the seminar, even though I was not a student yet. One time he had to attend a seminar at another school called Torch Trinity in Seoul, and he invited me to go with him. It was just him and me in the car, and we had a great time together. Professor Bondy was a gift from God. He was one person that really believed in me. Because of him, I was pushed to study the Word harder, and I tried to be a better person so that I would not let him down.

I mentioned Victor Marquez and his wife Katie from church. They often invited me to their house for a nice meal. We hung out together outside their home. I remember when we went to a quiz night. Our team was Victor, Katie, me and their friend Amy. I was not a very helpful member. I didn't even know what the questions meant half the time, like "What's the name of the day after Halloween?" Victor always said, though, that it was about us having fun rather than winning.

Amy was Katie's best friend. They were always together, so whenever they invited me to hang out, Amy was there too. We spent a lot of time together, and pretty soon Amy and I were hanging out by ourselves. And then we started liking each other. Amy was a little older than me, but it didn't matter. The more we spent time together, the more we wanted to spend even more time together.

Amy and I decided to go on a date at Mr. Pizza. This was my very first time eating at a restaurant in Korea, where I had to pay. Because of this, I had no idea how much anything cost. The date went well until I went to pay for our dinner. I discovered that the money I had was far less than the 20,000 won I now owed. I could not believe what I was seeing. Why did it cost that much? I made a mental note to check the prices before eating in the future. So I slowly pushed the bill to Amy and explained the problem to her. I imagine she was disappointed in me, because I hear, in America, if you go on a date the man has to pay. However, on this date the lady paid. It was embarrassing because, on this date, the man got the good treat. It was my first time at Mr. Pizza, and that Hawaiian Pizza was by far the best I had ever had. I walked Amy back home then I went back to my house. My first official date was over. But it went very wrong; I ate most of the pizza like a pig, and I did not pay for it. So I don't know if it really counts as a date.

As far as I could tell, things were going great. However, back at home the two gentlemen mentioned that they wanted me to start contributing a little bit toward the electric bill or rent. I was surprised by this, and I told them that there was no way I could contribute. Maybe, since I had told them about eating at Mr. Pizza, they thought that I had money to spend and just didn't want to contribute. It didn't help matters that their English was not very good and my Korean was awful. It was always hard to explain myself to them. I felt like a gap began to grow in our relationship. I could tell that I was starting to become more of a burden to them than a blessing. I ate their food, slept in their house, used electricity and water, and the only thing I gave back was a little help around the house.

I started to worry that these gentlemen would ask me to leave soon. In any foreign country, I think the most important thing is to have a place you can call home, but I felt I would be losing that soon. One night, no matter how much I did to talk or get feedback from them, they gave me the silent treatment. Things were quickly going south, and I was again wondering what God had for me next. In spite of the recent developments, I was still very thankful to these gentlemen for housing me, especially when I needed housing the most. I will be grateful forever.

The next morning I took a walk around the neighborhood as I prayed, and as I was walking around there was an older Korean man in the neighborhood. As I approached him, I smiled. The gentleman smiled back and stopped to talk to me. He told me his name, but I forgot it right away. His English was not very clear, but I understood that he was on a prayer walk to win that neighborhood for Christ.

He asked me whether I knew about Jesus Christ, and I told him that I was already a believer. I explained that I was also on a prayer walk, not for the neighborhood but for myself. I told him I was a long way from home, and I was in Korea following God's directions. The gentlemen asked where I was staying and I pointed to my apartment. He told me his church was not far from where I was staying. He asked for my phone number so that he could introduce me to a deacon at his church who spoke better English. This was good for me because I really wanted to make more connections in Korea. I gave him my phone number and told him that I would be waiting for the call.

Sure enough, the next day my phone rang and the caller told me that his name was Jo Mo. He was the deacon that the older gentleman had mentioned. Jo Mo spoke better English because he went to school in America. He was excited to meet up with me, so we set up a meeting time and place where he would pick me up to join him and his family for dinner at a restaurant. The awesome thing was that, though I was broke, somehow I still got a meal every day without begging. We talked over dinner and, like many people, he asked what my plans were. I told him that God would get me into school, but that otherwise I was just following where He led me. I guess the Spirit of God showed Jo Mo something that others did not see. He did not react negatively to me having no plan aside from following God's plan. As a matter of fact, he liked it so much that he wanted to introduce me to the rest of the leadership team at his church.

Jo Mo told his church's leadership team about me, and got his pastor's permission to invite me to their special leadership gathering that was a couple days away. For this gathering all the leaders met at a nice buffet restaurant. It worked out very well for me because I had all the time and appetite in the world. So, before Jo Mo finished asking me if I wanted to go, I knew my answer. He told me that a lot of people wanted to meet me, and he especially emphasized that the food was topnotch. That was all the motivation I needed to throw on my Sunday outfit and be ready to go. Jo Mo picked me up, and when we got there, it was the nicest restaurant I had ever been in. He was right to say the food was topnotch. There were all sorts of food, and I just couldn't wait for the pastor to finally say dig in.

Before the main pastor spoke I was asked to give a short greeting, and Jo Mo interpreted for me. Interestingly, the pastor's message that night was about how God called Abraham to leave his country and follow Him to a foreign land. As he preached he compared me to Abraham. He said, "This young man is on a journey for God like Abraham." He encouraged the leaders also to step out and obey God as they took the gospel to Korea and the world. I do not think that was coincidence that he had planned to speak about that topic the day I was visiting. Another person at that meeting came to me later and said, "You are a very blessed young man."

At the end of the dinner, I couldn't have eaten any more. It was the best Korean food I had had since arriving in Korea. During the ride back home, Jo Mo told me about Deacon Park, the man who had said I was a blessed young man. Jo Mo said this man wanted to know if there was a way he could help me while I stayed in Korea. I told him I would appreciate any help, and he said the deacon would pray more and seek God about how to help me. Within the week, Jo Mo called and said that deacon wanted to let me live in his home. He thought I would be a good influence on his son and even help him with his English.

This offer came at just the perfect time, considering the circumstances with the first two gentlemen. I accepted the deacon's offer, and I started making preparations to move out. Two days after I let the gentlemen know about my move, the deacon came over to pick me up. His house was bigger and better than the one I were I had been staying. Usually it was me, Deacon Park, his wife and his high school son. He had an older daughter, but she was stayed in the dormitory at her university.

Since I had a home that looked more permanent, and since I felt like Deacon Park would support me somehow with school, I tried really hard to get into Nazarene University. Since I was attending church there, the pastor and a lot of professors knew me. Even better, I met the president of the university. When I expressed my desire to join the school, his response was very positive. I had Deacon Park's family and Jo Mo convinced that I was going to get into the university, when the next semester began.

I applied and waited for results from the university, Deacon Park asked if I could help out at his shop while I waited for results. This would give me something to do and I would earn some money until school started. I also wanted to contribute, so that I did not just stay at his house doing nothing. He owned a shop in the fish market which supplied fish to many restaurants around Cheonan. My job was to go around with the truck driver delivering fish to the restaurants. I agreed, because it felt good to be able to give back something by helping his son with English at night and working at the fish market all day.

Every morning, we had to get up at about 3:30AM to make it to the early morning prayers. As far as I know, this is unique to Korean churches. I had never heard of it before. After the morning service we would go straight to work. We worked every day from 5AM to 7PM. In the delivery truck was me and an older gentleman. This man was not a Christian. He despised what I believed in, had a bad mouth and smoked like a chimney. What was worse was that I spoke zero Korean and he spoke no English, yet somehow we had to work together. He often got frustrated because I did not understand what he was saying to me, and he would yell and swear.

I didn't know what he was saying but I could tell it was bad by his facial expressions.

I did not mind helping out Deacon Park, but working with this guy was a nightmare which I always dreaded. I was exposed to smoke every day I worked with him, and pretty soon I started smelling like a smoker. He bossed me around a lot, and by the time I got home I was too tired to do anything. But at home Deacon Park's son wanted to play soccer, learn English and hang out with me. However, after the days I was having, I just wanted to lie down and sleep. As I worked I had less time for my friends at KNU and barely any time to hang out with Amy. I was getting so worn out.

By this time, it was December. This was without a doubt the coldest weather I had ever experienced. One evening I saw white stuff fall from the sky. It was not rain, and it was not an alien attack. It was snow. My country, Uganda, lies across the equator. We never see things like snow there. Watching the snow from the window looked great, but being in that snow all day was a nightmare. I felt like I was living in a freezer now. The only place I felt warm was inside a heated house. This first encounter with winter caused me to appreciate my African weather. Soon, I started to get very sick. I didn't want to get out of bed, let alone leave the warm house. Going to sleep was not fun because I worried about waking up so early the next morning. The nights started to feel short and shorter.

My body could not stand this weather, but I had to push myself every morning, because I wanted to give my best. I wanted to show my appreciation for Deacon Park. However, one morning the temperatures dropped even lower. I still got up in time for early service and work, but that day my body would not cooperate at all. I told the truck driver how I was feeling, but how I felt was the least of his concerns. All he wanted was to have the job well done. He yelled at me to move faster and work harder. I couldn't take it. I took off my gloves, and I told him that I was going home. I was too sick to work. He called Deacon Park, but he did not exactly explain the condition of my body. He said that I was lazy and did not want to work.

Deacon Park was very disappointed and I do not really blame him. Because of our language barrier, he called Jo Mo and told him what had happened. A few minutes later, Jo Mo called me. I told him exactly how I was feeling. I explained that working was not my problem. I really wanted to work and the job was not even that hard. The problem was the working conditions and the state of my body. Jo Mo told me a Korean philosophy. He said that, even if you feel sick, you have to keep working until you get better. He said he had never missed reporting in to work at church when he was sick. After this short speech, he encouraged me to go back to work.

I listened to what he told me and it made sense in my mind, but none of that made sense to my body. I was literally faced with a decision between my health and making Deacon Park happy. My body is the temple of the Holy Spirit. If I was going to risk my body that much, it was going to be for something better than selling fish, and it was going to be for God's Kingdom and not for man. I made up my mind. I loved Deacon Park and certainly appreciated all that he was doing for me. But I wanted to show my appreciation in some way other than selling fish. Koreans are some of the hardest working people I have ever met, so I understand why Deacon Park was disappointed.

Not working also meant that I would not be getting any money from Deacon Park. I sensed that I had caused a break in this relationship, too. I wanted to have the money, but it was not that important at the moment. I had seen God look out for me before without any money. As long as Deacon Park was willing to still provide me with shelter, I was alright. Thank goodness he did not kick me out of the house for not working, but his notion that I was lazy did not change. I stayed home when he and his wife went to work, and it was such a sweet feeling to fall asleep not worrying about an early wake up call. I spent more time with their son and more time at KNU with friends and with Professor Bondy.

Since I was staying at Deacon Park's house, I started going to his church. I was the first African ever to attend there. Fortunately, the service times were different, so I could continue attending the English worship at KNU. I went to the English worship 10AM and went to the Korean church at

1PM. The Korea church had an English youth service at 1PM, though most of the youths who attended spoke little English. They hoped to improve their English while they attended church. Jo Mo was in charge of this service. Most Sundays, he led worship while an American pastor usually came to preach.

I got so involved with this youth service that, one Sunday, I was asked to be the main preacher. That was the first time I preached in a service in Korea. A few people, some of whom rarely attended this service, came to hear me speak. It was a great opportunity for me to tell about God's goodness. Some people gave me positive feedback about how the message touched them. Many people at the church started calling me Abraham. After this, I was invited to more prayer meetings, and I met more young people with whom I built relationships.

The youth were planning to do a Christmas play for the whole church, and I was asked to be part of it. It seemed rather funny, since I could speak so little Korean, and what I could say sounded more like an African language than Korean. However, by this time I had learnt how to read Korean, thanks to my friend Jo Mo who took the time to teach me. They gave me the script for the play. I read and memorized the words, but I had absolutely no idea what I was saying. During rehearsals, my part took the most time. We had to repeat my parts over and over again, but at the end, I memorized my lines and was able to stand before the entire church and speak Korean for the first time in my life.

I have no idea if the words that came out of my mouth made any sense to the listeners, but they cheered loudest when I was on stage. I guess that was a good thing. After this play, I became a favorite for the kids. I believe I was the first African most of these kids had seen. They enjoyed teaching me Korean, and laughing whenever I failed to say the right thing. Every Sunday after church service the kids would ask their parents if they could remain behind and play with me. I had about fifteen kids around me every Sunday. They loved to touch my hair and have me chase them around.

After the Christmas play, I received a lot of feedback from the people who watched. Some thought my Korean was funny, and some could not believe an African young man was speaking Korea. Among the people I met was a newlywed couple; the wife was the main pastor's daughter. That night they invited all the play participants to go out for ice cream, so we all went downtown to Baskin Robbins. This was my first time trying this ice cream, and it was so unbelievably delicious. I was eating all these great things and I was thinking how ignorant my friends in Uganda were when they told me I would eat strange foods in Korea.

A week or two passed since I stopped working at Deacon Park's fish shop. Since I had no income but was spending on transport and food, I was quickly going broke. I do not know if it was pride, but I was determined not to beg people for money, even if I was broke. I wanted God to give me the money. I went to Korea Nazarene University, as it had become my daily routine. I had to leave the house every morning because Deacon Park's daughter was home for the winter break. She stayed in the house all day and everyone else was away. If only she and I were in the house, it did not look good. So I went to KNU every day and came back home at night. At lunchtime one day, I walked to the nearest McDonald's. However, when I got there, I just stood outside debating whether to use the little money I had on food or to skip the meal and save my money for other needs.

It was so hard to make a decision; it has always been hard for me to make decisions about not eating, so I was standing out there for some time. Sitting inside the restaurant was an elder gentleman who was watching me. I had no idea he was watching me until he waived his hand and caught my attention. I walked inside to find out why he waved at me. He smiled and introduced himself to me. He was Professor Randy, another English professor at KNU. He asked whether I was hungry and offered to buy my lunch that day. I was indeed very hungry, and I allowed him to buy me a Big Mac. Once again, I was able to save my money and eat at the same time without begging for food. God showed Professor Randy that I needed to eat. As we ate, he asked a lot of questions, and I told him a lot about myself. He took my phone number and said it would be great to keep in touch in the future, since I was planning to join the university.

I had so little money by this time, and even if I saved on food I still had to pay money to travel around and to keep my phone working. Even after breaking into my savings, I was down to about $2.

In the morning, I again went to KNU, but as I got off the bus my phone rang. It was Professor Randy. He asked if I could meet up with him, because he had something he wanted to give me. Since I was walking into the school as we spoke, I was able to meet him right away. We met up and he said, "Walk with me." We walked towards an ATM on campus. He withdrew $800 and gave it all to me as a gift. He said that he was simply following God's voice to provide for me.

When I talked to Professor Randy at McDonald's, I never told him that I was out of money, but somehow right at the moment when I was down to $2, he showed up and things changed instantly. One minute I was holding $2, and the next I had $800. I had never owned so much money in my entire life. This was too big for me, and I did not know how to react. I kept saying, "Wow, wow! I don't know what to say, Professor Randy!" I wanted to scream, I wanted to cry, I wanted to hug him. I had all sorts of emotions, but I looked up to heaven and praised God. I felt very rich. Walking back home that day I felt like I was being followed. I felt like I needed body guards. I thought now I could take Amy on a real date, buy a thank you gift for Deacon Park's family, and treat my friends to a meal, too. God was blessing me. I had made no plans for food, shelter and funds, but they all came.

I spent Christmas away from Uganda for the first time, and it was beautiful. Amy got me a small MP3 player, and since I had some money, I was able to buy some gifts, too. Christmas was made very special especially because of Amy, Victor and Katie. We spent the day together. They made a great meal. Even now, when I look at the pictures from that day, my eyes water up. It was special because they made me feel like family, like I belonged with them, regardless of where I came from. God was blessing me with friends and all the things I needed for staying in Korea.

Christmas was special, but several days after Christmas came my birthday. January 3, 2010 was the best birthday party I ever had. I spent the day with Katie, Victor and Amy because I knew they had plans to help me celebrate my birthday. I did not expect anything from Deacon Park's family. Honestly, I did not even want to tell them, because I still felt like they were disappointed in me for not working at the fish market.

After a great day with Victor, Katie and Amy, I got on the bus to go back home. I got off the bus and received a text message from Deacon Park's son asking me where I was. I told him that I was walking home. When I got off the elevator and opened the door, the lights were dim. I thought Deacon Park was already in bed; he usually went to sleep early, since he had to wake up so early every morning. I took off my shoes and walked into the house, and everyone screamed "Happy birthday!" His son held the cake while they sang Happy Birthday. They murdered the lyrics, but that did not matter. What mattered most was that they remembered my birthday, they probably spent time practicing the song, and they threw me my first surprise birthday party. I had tears in my eyes, as we ate the cake together. This was my best memory with Deacon Park's family.

The next day Jo Mo and his family invited me over to their house for another birthday party for me. Jo Mo's little son loved me; he never wanted to leave every time we hang out. He would cry whenever I left. On this night we played and ate, told stories and laughed. We had a great time.

I knew Jo Mo's name because it was easy to memorize. However, I had never called his wife by name. On this day, Jo Mo called her "Yobo" the entire time. I thought it was her name, but when I called her "Yobo," she seemed very shocked. And then she burst out into laughter. When Jo Mo came back to the room, she explained and he started laughing, too. I was confused, so I asked Jo Mo's wife to explain.

"My name is not Yobo," she said. "It means 'honey' in Korean and only a husband and wife use it."

It made perfect sense that they had laughed. But all in all it was a wonderful time, one of the few occasions I enjoyed getting older. Right after my birthday, though, I started worrying about my visa which would run out soon. I arrived in Korea in October with a three months tourist visa. Now it was January already. I had applied to Korea Nazarene University and turned in all my paperwork, but I still hadn't heard anything positive from the admissions office. I kept calling and they told me to wait.

Since KNU was my only option for extending my visa, I decided to visit the admissions office.

On this visit, I was told that many students had applied for scholarships, like me, and the students with a Nazarene denomination background got first priority. They suggested that I apply for the next semester.

I now had seven days until my tourist visa expired. Since I was so sure I would get into KNU, I had not applied anywhere else. Now I no chance of attending KNU, I was not ready to go back to Uganda, and I did not want to be an illegal immigrant in Korea. I was in a predicament; I was angry and confused, asking why God would let this happen to me. I was 100% sure that God would help me get into school in Korea, but after being rejected at Korea Nazarene University, I thought I was 100% wrong. I thought the voice I'd been hearing was not God. All my energy was sucked out of me; I tried so hard not to break down and cry. None of this made sense. I had met most of the professors who had influence in the school. Better yet, I had met the school's president with Professor Randy. I was already talking to Professor Bondy about the courses I was going to take. I was active in the Christian events on campus, so being rejected made zero sense.

I remember walking home that evening very depressed and hopeless, I had no idea how to tell Deacon Park, Jo Mo or all the people at church that had been praying for me to get into KNU. I felt shame in going back and telling all these people that our prayers did not work. I had told the Nesters, back in Uganda, that I would be getting into school at KNU and fulfilling the promise I made them to get back in school. But at that moment, I was faced with shame of telling them I could not get into the school and, worse, telling them that I would be deported soon. I had also told S that things were working out for me, God was blessing me, and I was about to be a student again. He was very excited for me, and he could not wait for the next time I would call to say I got into the university. I was not sure how to deliver this news to him.

I thought I was going through a very hard time, but it got worse. When I told Jo Mo and Deacon Park that I was not accepted into KNU, this seemed to worsen my relationship with Deacon Park. I do not blame him. I had stopped working for him, and now I was not going to be in school, so I was of very little value. Deacon Park called Jo Mo and told him that I should start thinking about moving out. When Jo Mo told me, it was like salt in my wound. I was already stressed about school, and now I had the stress of needing a place to live. I did not know who to talk to. As things were falling apart, I was also quickly losing friends.

I decided to talk to Amy. It was a Saturday, so I went to her home. She made lunch, we ate and watched a TV show called Smallville. We were seeing each other but we were not officially boyfriend and girlfriend yet. After an episode of Smallville, Amy said she wanted to tell me something. She paused the show, and told me she didn't think we should keep moving towards being boyfriend and girlfriend. She thought that things would not work between us, so she wanted to end it at that moment. Amy was the only person I thought I would have left even if everyone else left. By now I doubted whether anything would work in my favor.

I was wrong; something was working out in my favor. God was still on my side even when it seemed like everyone I trusted seemed to turn their back on me. I questioned whether God was calling me to Korea, but as I was crying in my room, in my heart I could hear God say, "What must I do for you to believe in me?" God was God in my life before I even knew KNU; He was God when I lost all my friends. In that difficult time I needed to look up to heaven, and be still and know that He was still God in my life. He was God regardless of what thing were or were not working out, and ultimately everything would work out for my good. I have had moments like this when I have to preach to myself and wipe away my own tears.

God was going to do His work in me even if everyone I knew in Cheonan decided to leave me. God was capable of using someone else. Like Mordecai told Esther,

"For if you remain silent at this time, relief and deliverance for the Jews will arise from another place, but you and your father's family will perish. And who knows but that you have come to your royal position for such a time as this?" (Esther 4:14) Esther was the queen, and she was in a far better position to help, but God did not need her. In the same way, I met people who had the resources to help me, but God did not need them. If they chose not to help, help was going to arise from another place. I did not give up my desire to attend university. If KNU rejected me, admission would come from another university. God gives people an opportunity to serve, but He does not need them. God even used a donkey to speak in the Old Testament. He WILL accomplish is will.

I needed to hold on to God and remember that I came this far not because of KNU or anyone but God. So I went to God in prayer, and asked Him to show me the way. That night, after praying, I felt in my heart that I should visit Seoul. I had no idea why I was going to Seoul, I had no plans, but I knew that I needed to go. So the next morning I got on the train for Seoul. This was my first time to take a train by myself; I was afraid of taking the wrong train or just missing my train. Luckily, I saw another black man on the subway, and I ran to him like I knew him. We talked and I learned that he had been in Korea for longer, and we were getting on the same train. He was African too, from Angola. As we talked, he asked why I was going to Seoul, and I told him I was just going. So he recommended that I visit a place called Itaewon.

When I left the house I had no idea exactly where I was going, but after this man recommended Itaewon, I determined that was where I would go. We arrived at Seoul Station, and the African gentleman and I parted ways. But before he left he gave me clear directions to Itaewon from Seoul Station. Right after I got off the subway at Itaewon Station, a Nigerian man began talking to me. I know this sounds bad, but I had been warned about Nigerian men. So, with that in mind, I was very skeptical. What this man wanted from me? However, I did not own much, so I had littke to lose. To my surprise, he offered to buy me lunch at the KFC right outside the station.

My unfounded fear about this man really stood in the way of me ministering to him or appreciating the fact that he was trying to help me. We walked into KFC and he bought the meal. As we ate I kept waiting him to say, "This is what I need you to do in return for the meal." But when finished eating, he stood up and told me he had to go back to his business. I was very amazed, and I felt guilty for stereo-typing this man. He was at the subway right as I got off, as if he was waiting for me, and he bought me a meal. Even better, he referred me to a place where he had seen a Ugandan woman. Could it be that God had that gentleman out there actually waiting for me?

A few minutes after he left, I decided to go to the place where he said I would find the Ugandan woman. It was not in my plans to go meet anyone, but I went. I found the place, and she was there, we talked. She offered me a cup of tea, and welcomed me to Seoul. The funny thing, though, was that it seemed she was expecting me to visit. Somehow the conversation led to the visa issue that I faced. Then she told me that people who, for different reasons, can't go back to their countries can apply for refugee status in Korea. However, she said it was not that easy. Korea is a small country and many people, especially from the Middle East, China and South East Asia, had already applied for refugee status here. In other words, it would be hard for a Ugandan to apply and be granted refugee status. I told her that I was not ready to go back to Uganda, and I was going to try applying. It was already getting late, so she allowed me to stay in her small house for the night. In the morning I would visit the immigration office.

While I lived with the Nesters, I started a habit of praying every morning before I even stepped out of my bed. Part of my prayer was that today God would put someone in my way that I could minister to or that would minister to me. I was asking God to reveal Himself to me on a daily basis through the people I encountered. So from then on, I stopped viewing meetings with people as random or coincidence but as an opportunity to share the love of God.

We live in a broken world. It is full of broken relationships, broken families, broken hearts and people dealing with all sorts of pain, deaths, diseases, hunger, poverty, loneliness, misery, and more. There are children around the world who have no father or mother; they walk around seeking for a father figure. People are looking for hope. Many people have been told they are not good enough, and they don't measure up to the world's standards for beauty or intelligence or wealth. Some people have no one to turn to; even their families mistreat them. On the outside they look calm, but on the inside they are crying out for someone to come and bring hope into their lives. I know because I am one of those people. That day I travelled to Seoul looking for hope. I was blessed to find some people who were not too busy to help me. However, there are many who walk around crying for hope, but no one hears them. Everyone is too busy with their own lives.

Hurting people get on the same buses and subways that we take, and they pass us on the streets. They might even have said hi to us the morning before they committed suicide. They go to the same coffee shops and the same restaurants where we go. We might think someone is just rude or doesn't want to talk, but maybe keeping silent is the only way that person manages to keep the pain contained. Even people in church, leaders and congregation members, are broken. We have people among us dealing with all sorts of stuff and they cry out for hope. Can anyone hear them?

In Uganda, because a lot of people do not use electricity, candles are commonly used. I have heard stories about parents leaving their kids at home. Maybe the kids fell asleep, but something catches fire from the candles and the fire spreads and kills the children. One of the most common things neighbors would say is, "Maybe the kids cried out and screamed for help, but we were too busy to hear them." In the same way, people around us are crying out, but we are preoccupied with our stuff and we cannot hear them. So they slowly are destroyed right before our eyes.

"And when Jesus had stepped out of the boat, immediately there met him out of the tombs a man with an unclean spirit. He lived among the tombs. And no one could bind him anymore, not even with a chain ... Night and day among the tombs and on the mountains he was always crying out and cutting himself with stones" (Mark 5:2-5).

This man is like those I talked about above. He lived alone among the tombs, and usually the tombs are only a place for dead people. The Bible says "no one could bind him anymore." I suppose this man, every now and then, would go into the city. But he was too messed up. He probably bothered people who were trying to work, so they would tie him up and throw him out of the city. He was miserable, he was hurting, and he was living among the dead. He cried out for nights and days among the tombs and mountains, but I bet no one could hear him, no one lived in the tombs or mountains.

One day this demon possessed man was going to cry for the last time, he was going to cut himself for the last time, because that day the savior who would hear this man's cry, who would cast all the unclean spirits was passing by that day. And when Jesus saw the demon possessed man, he cast the demons out of him and the entire village witnessed this miracle. Furthermore the demon possessed man came to Christ's saving knowledge that day.

There might be a purpose for running into the people we see throughout the day. We should ask God to use us to minister to the "random" people we meet. On that day, we might be the only Jesus they get to see. We might be the only hope they receive to not give up on life. Every day we ought to walk in the mind of wanting to serve God and making every day count. Every time we step out of our houses we step into a mission field and we should use every opportunity for His glory. Every time Jesus stepped out He served, even to the demon-possessed man living among the graves.

If you pray and walk daily in the same mind of service as Jesus, God will open your eyes to see all those that are hurting and needing to taste God's love. God will open your ears to hear the cries of many whom no one can hear. Pray for God to show these people to you. Maybe the next time someone bumps into you, you will not curse at them but pray for them. Maybe the next time someone stares at you or tries to talk to you, you will not call the police or run away from them, because that day you might be the only Jesus that they see. Do not waste that moment. When I walked out of the Itaewon subway, I was walking out with no direction. I needed someone to buy be a meal and point me in the right direction. And there was someone to minister to me in just that way.

Maybe you are reading, and you are the one who is hurting and looking for hope. Jesus hears your cries. Though people might count you out, though it might feel like you are crying alone, Christ is right there to wipe your tears away and turn your mourning into joy. I cried and wept, and my only comfort came from my Lord Jesus Christ. *Matthew 11:28 "Come to me, all who labor and are heavy laden, and I will give you rest"*

I spent the night at the Ugandan lady's house and early in the morning I went to the immigration office and explained my situation to them. I told them that I never wanted to be an illegal immigrant, but I was not ready to go back to my country. I know it sounds unbelievably easy, but just like that I was given a temporary visa to stay in Korea until they called me back to the immigration office. Then it finally made sense why God had me travel to Seoul; my visa worries were put to rest for now. This was the hope I was looking for, and God used a couple of random people to help me get there. Dealing with visas is no easy task, but God made it look very easy for me at that time. Glory to His Holy name!

After immigration I got on the train to head back to Cheonan, I was in such a good mood, and I felt bad for doubting God. I got home in the evening and Deacon Park's wife was already at home with her son, but she was very angry. So I asked the son what the problem was, and he told me I was the problem. I had spent the night in Seoul without their permission. I had told the son I was going to Seoul, and I thought he would tell his parents. I don't blame her for being angry, because I was living under her roof and I had to play by the rules at her house.

I noticed that Korean parents, when they are angry, are not very different from Ugandan parents. She asked me questions as if she needed answers, but when I started talking she would say, "Don't talk back to me." My mother used to do the same thing; if I spoke I was wrong, and if I kept quiet I was wrong for ignoring her. After that they called Jo Mo, who was always the middleman, and they told him again I needed to think about moving out.

I think my trip to Seoul this was just the tip of the iceberg from all the other things, like not working for them and not being able to get into school. This time I was sure where my help came from, so I went to my room and prayed to God for a couple of hours. My prayer changed, too. I was not telling God that I was scared of being homeless or being kicked out. Instead I was asking God to show me what was next and which direction I needed to go. After prayer I laid down to sleep peacefully waiting for God to speak. After a few minutes I was led to call someone in Seoul. I had no idea who that person was, and I definitely did not have their phone number. I got out of bed, went to the internet, and found Pastor Bill Major's phone number. I thought this was the person God wanted me to call. I called him and asked him if I could visit his church on Sunday. Of course he said yes, and the next morning on Sunday I was on the train back to Seoul to see Pastor Bill Majors.

This time I was sure to ask for permission from Deacon Park before I went to Seoul. I got permission, so I took the train to Seoul. I was supposed to go to Myeong-Dong where Pastor Bill Major's YongNak Church is located. I had written down the directions Pastor Bill had given me, however, something was wrong with the directions. I got lost a little bit but eventually I found my way to the church. I arrived at YongNak Church right before the 3PM service began. I went into the church, and sat in the back until the service was over. Pastor Bill did something special; he gave the benediction from the entrance to the church and not from the pulpit. In this way he was able to get to the door before anyone else, and he was able to greet everyone as they walked out of church. Pastor Bill had no idea what I looked like, but he shook my hand and said, "You are new here." I told him that it was my first time here and thanked him for inviting me.

He wondered when he invited me, and I explained that I had called him from Cheonan the previous night.

He remembered that I called him, and his smile grew even bigger. He asked whether it was easy to find my way, and I told him I had a little trouble with the directions, but the most important thing was that, by God's grace, I arrived at church on time. He held onto my hand, and asked me if I could stay behind and chat with him more after he greeted everyone. Of course I wanted to stay and talk to him, because I also wanted to find out why God had me call this person. After he greeted everyone, he told me to walk with him to his office. We got to the office and he said, "Young man, there is something special about you, would you tell me more about yourself?"

I told him the entire story. By the time I finished I could see tears in his eyes. "You are like a very beautiful pearl, Emmanuel!" I believe that God was working on Pastor Bill and preparing him to meet me. That was why He gave me Pastor Bill's number.

After talking with Pastor Bill that evening, he asked me if I would stay the night and spend time with him more the next morning. I told him I wouldn't mind at all, so he fed me and found a place for me to stay at YongNak Church. I got up early that morning very excited to hang out with Pastor Bill. He picked me up from the church early the next morning. He said he wanted me to meet a friend of his, and he asked whether I knew football. Of course I did, since I had played football since I was a small boy. But he and I were talking about very different things. He was talking about American football. I still do not understand why that game isn't called "throw ball" or "handball." I suspect many soccer players think the same way. Anyway, that morning was special because it was the Super Bowl. He said it was like the World Cup finals.

I had seen the Nesters watch it, but I'd had zero interest in this game aside from admiring how big and strong those players were. I was excited to see this game, though. We drove to the US army base in Yongsan where we watched the game. The game was boring to me, but the atmosphere was great. Many Americans were gathered together to watch the game. The overall atmosphere on the army base felt very different from that off base. We were joined by an older man, the person Pastor Bill wanted me to meet. He was Pastor Bill's mentor and old friend, Ken Werho. Like Pastor Bill, Ken Werho had lived in Korea for a very long time, and he was also attending YongNak Church. The Pittsburg Steelers won the game, but who really won? After the game Ken offered to buy us lunch, so we walked down to the food court. When we got there, I saw a variety of good looking American food. It brought back memories of what Jonah used to tell me, and I knew I would have a lot of trouble determining just one meal that I wanted to eat.

I took my time to exploring my options. As I looked around I saw something that looked like McDonald's except that it looked better. This place was called Burger King. One glance at Burger King was all I needed. This was what I was going to have for lunch. Call this love at first sight! The burgers on the picture cried out, "Come and get me! If you miss this chance, shame on you." I know I tend to get a little too excited when it comes to food. There was a time in my life when I did not have food to eat, so when I see food, I really do get excited. I ordered a triple whopper, the largest burger on the menu. When I placed my order, Ken's expression showed he doubted whether I could finish it. When my meal was ready, I was so fast to pick it up. In three minutes at most, that big burger was reduced to nothing but a few vegetables that I did not want to eat. The entire time Ken stared at me tearing up that burger. I was done before they were even halfway through their meal.

To this day Ken is one of my favorite people in Seoul. We still meet up and eat good food together, particularly On the Boarder, a steak restaurant, and many more that I usually could not afford if not for Ken. He knows how much I love to eat, so every now and then he calls and asks whether I want to eat. I have never said no. Ken introduced me to Burger King and for that our friendship will forever live on. As I look back, it seems like burgers have played a great role throughout my life. I had another special Burger King moment to bond with the Pereas, a special family in Korea. I coached their son's soccer team, and I spent a lot of time with their son,

Danny, working on his soccer skills. They took me to Burger King and watched me destroy a triple and double whooper in one sitting.

After Super Bowl day lunch, Pastor Bill and I left Ken on base and went our way. We stopped at church again and talked more about my future and what I was hoping to do. I told Pastor Bill that I was here on God's directions and I was just following Him. Pastor Bill then expressed his desire for me to join his church. He also expressed a desire to support me, starting with shelter. I thought I was dreaming, but this was happening. In only two days God gave me the support that I needed to carry on. I did not need to worry about being homeless, because God was in control. So I told Pastor Bill that I would go back to Cheonan and wrap up there. Then I would move to Seoul and start going to YongNak Church.

On my way back to Cheonan, and I was full of praise. God was opening doors and making ways where no way seemed to exist. When I got to Cheonan, I told Deacon Park, Jo Mo and other close friends that I would be moving to Seoul, but I wanted to attend church in Cheonan one last time. So I set my date of departure to Sunday right after the morning worship at the Korean Church. At church I was given a grand farewell. I expressed my appreciation to Jo Mo, Deacon Park and all the people who helped me in Cheonan. Some of the kids I played with every Sunday cried. Some people told me YongNak was a huge church in Korea with a huge reputation, and they thought God was opening up a bigger door for me to serve Him. I received their blessings and, like that, the Cheonan chapter of my life ended and a new chapter began in Seoul.

CHAPTER 24

JOURNEY TO SEOUL

On the train to Seoul, I had time to meditate and think about God's goodness, how He was blessing me in a foreign land, and I was in tears. I arrived at YongNak Church and this time I was coming to attend the church as a member not a mere visitor. Pastor Bill encouraged me to step out and meet new people and make friends. The first people I befriended were Chris Coupland, Wade Hawkins, and Richard Moore. Later I met Cory Dyck, who is still one of my best friends.

Pastor Bill had a friend named David Abram Milanaik who was away on vacation; he left the key to his house with Pastor Bill. Pastor Bill asked David about letting me stay at his house for a little while as I figured out my next step. David was kind enough to let me stay. I met Pastor Bill again the next day to sit down and make plans about my future. Like many people before him, Pastor Bill asked me about my plans. And I gave the same answer I had given to everyone else; I planned to get into school and I was following God's directions.

Pastor Bill told me that I was not very different from him, and then he told me his story of how he came to Korea. In his twenties, he felt God leading him to move to Korea. So he came on a one way ticket, and with very little money to spend. Just like me, Pastor Bill wanted to get into school in Korea, which he was able to do, and through his years in Korea, he became fluent in Korean and made a lot of friends along the way. So when I expressed my desire to become a student, Pastor Bill told me that he would talk to one of his friends at Myongji University. Pastor Bill talked to his friend, Chaplain Koo Jae Hong.

Chaplain Koo could not get me into the University but he talked to the school's president about giving me a full ride scholarship. I was waiting as I prayed for God to make a way for me. Two days later, Pastor Bill called to say the President of Myongji University wanted to meet me. I dressed up in my special church clothes to go meet the president of Myongji. This was special to me, because it was a big step toward becoming a student again. However, I refused to get carried away because I had met a university president before and still failed to be accepted. I went to church to meet up with Pastor Bill, and then we drove to Myongji. We first went to Chaplain Koo's office, and then Chaplain Koo walked with us to the president's office. By this time and I was very nervous, but I had to remain calm, and I asked God to give me favor at that particular time. The president asked me some questions, and I tried to answer them the best I could.

The president said he was very impressed and he went on to say that he would grant me a full ride scholarship to study at Myongji University. However I had to go through the Korean Language Program first. I could only become a full time student after I learnt the Korean language, so I had a full ride scholarship and all I had to do was study hard. Right at that moment I wanted to scream and dance, but I worked hard to stay calm till I got back to my room. I could not wait to tell the Nesters about this and to fulfill the promise I made to them. I was very happy to know that the voice I was listening to was God's voice. He promised to put me back in school and He did it. When I told someone in Cheonan about being admitted into Myongji University, he said I should be glad because Myongji is ten times better than KNU.

After he said that I remembered what Pastor Terry always told me. "Emma, God wants the best for you. Never settle for good." God wanted the best for me, and He wanted Myongji, not KNU. I think that, many times, we settle for good when God wants the best for us. I was really upset when I was not accepted into KNU. If I known that God had a better university in mind for me, I would have been thankful instead of crying. When God gives us gifts, He gives us the very best. He gave us His only Son to die on the cross for our sins. His gifts to me have enabled me to do more in Seoul than in Cheonan as far as ministry and my life are concerned

Sometimes we fear that our current opportunity might be our only one. Even if it is just a mediocre opportunity, it is easy to jump on it instead of waiting or seeking God's guidance about it. I have heard so many people say they are in a horrible relationship, but if they get out of it they think it will be hard to find someone else. They fear being alone. Some people are stuck in terrible jobs, but they are not about to change because they also fear that they will not find anything better. Whatever it is we can never settle for good. God wants the best for us, and He has the best for us. I think, many times, the reason we do not receive God's best is that we are so willing to settle for less. Like Thomas Merton said, "the biggest human temptation is to settle for too little."

I look at it as being offered a delicious piece of cake but only eating the crumbs. For example, the Bible says, "He who finds a wife finds a good thing and obtains favor from the LORD" (Proverbs 18:22). Some translations say that he finds a "treasure." When a lady settles for a man who does not treasure her, she settles for the crumbs. A treasure is incredibly valuable thing to you. You guard it well, you handle your treasure with care, you will love it and it comes before everything else. Tragically, many women are abused—physically, verbally and emotionally. They are just being used, not treasured. It is very sad when people settle for these kinds of relationships and miss out on the best. Not only relationships, but in all we do, we should strive for the best because that is what God has in store for us.

CHAPTER 25

MYONGJI UNIVERSITY

The day I had dreamt of for a very long time had arrived. I was fully admitted into Myongji University. Orientation ended and I started my study Korean language classes. I moved from David's house into the university dorm. For the language program, I took classes for four hours every day Monday through Friday. Since YongNak Church was helping me, I spent all day Sunday serving at the church and sometimes went on Saturdays. My school expenses were covered by the scholarship, and YongNak provided money for me shelter and food.

As I settled into Seoul, opportunities came for me to testify for God. The first was at Seoul Foreign School. Most of the students there were Christians. They had different Bible study groups throughout the semester, and occasionally the entire student body gathered together to hear from a special speaker. This time around I was the speaker. I was very nervous, but I stood up to speak God's word. Based on feedback from some of the students and teachers who attended, God's word touched many hearts.

Soon after that, Pastor Bill put me in charge of the youth worship at church. I liked this a lot because I felt like I had a sure opportunity to impact the youth at my church. This is what really brought joy in my life, to know that I was serving God, and that Pastor Bill gave me an opportunity to serve in IWE. YongNak is a huge Korean Church and Pastor Bill led the International Worship in English (IWE). I spent time studying and preparing to pour into the lives of these young people. And it gave me great joy to see that I was positively impacting them. I was encouraged when their parents told me I was doing a great job. While I led the youth group I also helped with media for the church and sometimes with the children's Sunday school.

Pastor Bill asked me to share my testimony with the church one Sunday. It was a great opportunity to talk about God's goodness to me and to let explain a little bit more about me. We had services at 10AM 3PM, and I was able to share my testimony in both services. We usually posted the services online. To my surprise, many months later, someone approached me at church.

"I am new in Korea," he explained. "I watched your story and I thought I would visit the church so that I could meet you." It was a good thing to hear. Even people outside my church got to hear my story.

I was told that I was the first African student ever to join Myongji University. The first month was tough, but funny at the same time. First, I was just very excited to be a student again, but also I experienced a lot of the stereotypes that Koreans have about black people. It started from the first day I was in the dorm. When the dorm caretakers learned that I was coming from Uganda, I guess they imagined a big village with no electricity and animals and naked people running around, like in the movie *The Gods Must Be Crazy*. Therefore, when I first arrived in the dorm, the guard gave a special orientation, just for the African student. He taught me how to use the elevator and correctly press the numbers. So if I was going to the fourth floor, I had to press the number four button in the elevator. If I didn't do that I would get lost. He asked me to try it out by myself and I passed with flying colors. It is funny being taught how to use an elevator when you already know. Then he taught me how to turn the lights on and off. We went to the washing machines, but he thought that would be too much for me to memorize, so he said to just call him if I needed to do laundry. I love this man. He became a very good friend. I would stop by his office once in a while to talk. I miss those days joking around with him.

Everyone in class was from Asia except me. Every now and then, in class, I would catch the teacher starring at my head trying to figure out what the deal was with my hair. The students would laugh at my pronunciation of Korean words. I was so accustomed to the Ugandan culture of saying hi or waving, and I often forgot that the proper greeting here was to bow to my professors. Sometimes I would bow and wave at the same time, but my professors were gracious with me. I was used to being free with the teachers. In Africa it was helpful to learn if you were comfortable with the teachers. I learnt that here I had to keep a good distance from the teachers. In this culture, it sounded very strange if I asked my professor to have lunch with me. I was learning fast.

Sometimes, while walking down the hallway, a couple of students would run to me and ask me if I knew Tupac or Eminem. They would ask me to rap for them, but where I come from we do not rap. We play drums and sing Ugandan music. When I told these students I did not know how to rap, they did not believe me. One once said, "But you look like Jay Z. How come you cannot rap?" Back in my room I found Jay Z's picture online; we do not look alike at all. Later, I was compared to another rapper. Maybe to these students, all black people look alike. Since I would not rap for anyone, some people thought I was shy or unfriendly. The truth was I could not rap, even to save my life.

I would be a hypocrite to be upset with these students, because I did the same thing. Most of my classmates in my language class were Chinese, and based on the Chinese movies I watched, I thought all Chinese people were really good at Kung Fu. I seriously thought these students were Kung Fu professionals, and maybe they would teach me something about Jackie Chan fighting techniques. To my surprise, most had never even tried Kung Fu before. I probably knew more Kung Fu from the Jackie Chan movies than most of my classmates did. When they got into fights, there were never any Kung Fu moves. They just yelled at each other, and I was very disappointed (don't judge me). I just wanted to see some live action. So I understood a little why they expected me to rap because I was black.

On a couple occasions, some students walking towards me would intentionally wear their hats sideways or backward to show me that they were cool. Some would change their walk to have a little bounce in it. A couple other students, when they saw me, would start to rap in broken English. It was very funny.

In all the schools I previously attended, I was always active in sports, especially soccer. It was not easy to play soccer at Myongji because I did not have that many friends with whom to play. I decided to check out basketball, since it was easier to do pickup games of basketball than soccer. The first time I came to the court, I could see excitement in the eyes of many students. I was not even there to play that day; I just wanted to watch, but they insisted I play. Every time I got the ball, all eyes were on me. They expected me to do something special, and some yelled, "Dunk the ball!" But if you have met me, you know that I am not very blessed with height, so telling me to dunk was a funny suggestion. They called me names like Jordan and Iverson, and I felt so much pressure to perform. It became hard to play because I did not want to disappoint these students who had such high expectations for me.

Crazily enough, there were pickup games in which I actually played center, because I jumped higher than most people I played with. Back in Uganda I was too short to even play point guard. My friends joked about how short I was. E Even when I was standing on my toes, they would say, "Stand up. We cannot see you!" Jonah would stand next to me and ask, "Where is Emma?" Only while playing basketball in Korea have I jumped higher than people taller than me! I loved it. But a couple of times I have been humbled when I drive in like a big man and have my shots blocked. Somehow I was crazy enough to think I could actually dunk it, and I came up way short. But all in all, I've had a lot of fun times on that basketball court. It is one of my favorite places on campus.

Before S and I parted ways, back in Busan, I had promised that I would call him to give him a testimony of how God had taken care of me. After I made it into Myongji University I called him and I reminded him of my promise. I told S that I was a student at a prestigious University in

Seoul called Myongji. I had a full ride scholarship through school. I was serving in a good church. Shelter was not a problem for me anymore. I had financial support from my church. I was going out to schools like Seoul Foreign School and Centennial Christian High School to share the gospel. I had made a lot of great friends. And I could say a few sentences in Korean. S wanted to see with his eyes, so I invited him to come. I showed him around the church and school, and I bought him dinner. Then I asked him, “Do you believe now?” He replied, “Emma, now I believe. I believe God can do anything.” S knew my struggles, but again He witnessed how God turned things around.

After about two months, things started to settle down at school. People figured out that I am not a good rapper, and I was never going to dunk the basketball for them. One experience, though, was very bad. Because my English was better than most of the Korean students, many people thought I was an American. Some students wanted to be friends with “the American guy” on campus. For some reason, they attached a lot more value to Americans, so I lost friends when they found out that I was actually Ugandan. I did my own test; often the very first thing people asked me was where I was from. If I said I was from Uganda, many people showed no interest and the conversation ended. However, if I said I was from America, they generally showed more interest and wanted to be my friend. This did not really bother me, since I was not in Korea to follow God, not to be liked by people. As long as He approved, I was all good.

First semester, I was one of the worst students. Korean was a lot harder for me than it was for the Japanese and Chinese students in my class. Their languages have much more in common with Korean. Sometimes I was scared to give my answers because I thought one of the other students had a better answer to give. I thought I would be wrong, and they would laugh at me. Things never made sense to me as well as they did for the other students. I always slowed the class down with my unending questions, but my teachers were very understanding. My performance was not the best, but I was improving. At one point I was the A class for smart students, class was divided into three and A was for the best students. This might be normal for some, but to me it was such a blessing that God could let me learn this foreign language and even do better than some Asian students whose native languages have some similarities with Korean.

After completing the Korean Language Class, in allow to be allowed in as a fulltime student, I had to pass the final university entrance exam. When I met the university president, he promised me a full ride scholarship if I successfully completed the Language program. That meant that I had to study hard and pass my final university entrance exams. Truthfully, if you asked people back then which students stood a chance of getting into the university, my name would not have be on the list. They were very right, I could not do it in my own strength, but I was not depending on my own capabilities. I was depending on God to help me pass this exam. We took the test, and when the results came back, my name was third on the list of students who made it. Glory to God! Now, that four-year full scholarship was mine.

While I was taking language course, I was still on the temporary visa I got right before moving to Seoul. That visa allowed me to take language classes, but no I needed to get a student visa. So I had the scholarship, but I did not have the visa needed to start school. In order to cancel that visa, I had to leave the country and come back on the student visa. The only problem was that, if I left the country there was no guarantee I was going to come back. I could be given the student visa or not be given the visa. But I couldn't get it without leaving the country. It felt like I was jumping off a cliff and hoping that God would stretch out His hands and grab me before I reached the ground.

It seemed very hard, but again it was one of those times where God was calling me to trust Him and remember how He had taken care of me before. I went to Hong Kong because I did not need a visa to go there. Before I left Seoul, I tried to make contacts in Hong Kong. I sent out emails to churches, tried to talk to people. I wanted to know someone before I got there. The few people who replied said I might be a scam, so I had no contacts at all. I thought it made sense that, if I reached out to churches, they would want to help me. I guess I was wrong. I had no idea how long it was going to take to process my visa, so I had no idea how long

I would be in Hong Kong. I was hoping for a very short visit, because I did not have enough money to survive for long.

Daniel Fertig, a member of IWE, travelled often for work and had enough points for a free night's stay at Marriot Hotel. He gave that free stay to me for my Hong Kong trip. This was my first time to sleep in a hotel, and it was such a nice one! The only problem was that I only had one night to sleep in that soft bed; waking up in the morning was very hard. But I had to get up early that morning and go to the Korean Embassy. I went to the Korean Embassy the next morning, but it was closed for the day. I would have to go back the next business day. Small things like this tend to discourage me; the one day that I decided to visit the embassy was the time it took a day off. My night at the Marriot was finished. I was on my own with the little money that the church had given to me.

This was not my first time to have no friends or money, and everything worked out because God was with me. I asked God to lead me and bring people in my life like He had done when I was in Korea with no friends. I felt Him telling me to visit a church called ECC. I got to the church that night with my luggage, and I spoke with a Filipino lady named Riza Barrera Guevarra. I explained my situation and asked if I could spend the night at the church. She was just one of the helpers at the church, and she could not make decisions like that, so she told me that was not possible. When she said no, I asked if I could at least leave my luggage in a storage room for the night. She said she could not make that decision either. We both stood there in silence. I had come here with some confidence that I was going to stay at this church because that is what God put on my heart. However, it did not look that way, based on this conversation with Miss Barrera.

After minutes of silence, she told me to wait while she talked to someone else. She called Lucy, the lady in charge of missions. Miss Barrera explained my situation, and Lucy told her to buy me dinner and let me leave my luggage at church. On top of that, Lucy said that she would drive from her home to the church to meet me in person. While we ate dinner, Miss Barrera told me that Lucy was coming and was excited to meet me. We finished dinner and walked back to church. Lucy was waiting for us. She greeted me and told me she was praying on her way drive over; it was okay for me to stay at the church. I was shown a very nice room where I would spend the night. The only thing Lucy told me was, "Don't party too hard." This blew my mind. In the normal world, you do not just give a stranger access to a church full of expensive stuff. Besides, Africans do not have the best reputation, but she trusted me in the very short time she met me.

The next day was Sunday. As I walked out of the room, I met a couple people from the morning youth service. It was led by Pastor Marcus. I met Pastor Marcus and I introduced myself, and soon a couple more young people joined us. I told them that I was from Uganda, and they told me that they had just come back from a mission trip in Rwanda. They said it was life changing. They asked me why I was in Hong Kong, so I gave them a quick version of the story. They gave me such a great welcome, as if I was a visitor they expected to have. Jonathan Lau, who was also on ECC staff, told me that he had friends who had gone to school in Kenya, and these friends were currently in Hong Kong. He told me the name of their school was Rift Valley Academy in Kijabi. I was surprised because I knew that school; I had friends who had attended that school.

Jonathan called these friends, Hannah and Jonathan Lai, and told them about me. They came to the church to meet me. We even discovered some mutual friends, Zach Bissett and Hannah Kingsbury. Before I left Seoul I tried so hard to make contacts in Hong Kong. I had been frustrated by my lack of success, but God had a better plan. In one short morning I made several friends. Jonathan Lau invited me to stay at his house for the rest of my time in Hong Kong. My new friends also provided a meal every day for me, but the best part was the fellowship I enjoyed around these young people. This was the most active young adults group that I had ever encountered. I enjoyed playing soccer or basketball every night with them. Once we all went to the beach for a cook out. That fun day is one my all-time favorite moments in life. Seeing how strong this youth group was gave me a desire to reach out to the young adults in Seoul. I wanted to create a family for them like the young people at ECC had. I developed a new passion to reach out to young people. Now I just needed to be able to get back to Seoul.

Also, that Sunday, there was a special speaker named Morgan Jackson. He worked for an organization called Faith Comes By Hearing (FCBH). This organization provides audio scriptures to people around the world in their mother tongue. After the young adults' service I went to listen to Pastor Jackson. But after he finished preaching, he called for me out of the crowd. He asked where I was coming from, and what I was doing. I do not know if God showed him something or if I just stood out. He gave me his business card and asked me to contact him or partner with him to take the oral gospel to my people in Uganda. It was not my time yet to go back to Uganda, though. There was still work God wanted to do in me and through me in Korea. Still, it was amazing the way things were happening.

The next morning, I went back to the Korean Embassy. Thank God, it was open this time. I let the official know why I was visiting, but her reply hit me a bomb. She said that, since I was not a Hong Kong citizen, I needed to go to Uganda to get a visa to get back into Korea. I was starting to wonder why things never go smoothly with me. Why can't I just walk in and get the visa without complications? But when I look back, it was those moments when I was weakest, that the power of God was manifested in my life. Again I prayed. I needed to go back to Korea and start life as a full time student. I didn't have money to go all the way back to Uganda for the visa. I had to get the visa from Hong Kong.

The lady went into another room with my papers, and when she came back she was a different person. She had a smile on her face, and she told me to pay for the visa and come back in three days later to pick up my passport. God stretched out His arms and grabbed me again. God has the power over any issues in our lives. Within three days, I received a new student visa, and I was legally recognized as a full time undergrad student. Glory to The Most High God!

Now that I had the visa, I set my date for returning to Korea. Now I had one vision in my mind: to impact young people in Korea for Christ. As soon as I got back, I began with a movie night at YongNak Church. This was meant to bring young adults together for food, fun and Christian fellowship. We watched a movie, played board games and ate pizza. My goal was to create was a family of young believers who could encourage each other and bring each other closer to Christ. Some other things we did together were hiking, watching sports, and dining out.

I saw the need for the church to step up and help young adults in Seoul, especially the foreigners. Many foreigners leave their homes and churches to work or study in Seoul. During this time away from their biological and spiritual families, some foreigners have a hard time finding family in Seoul like they had back at home. When I was stuck in Hong Kong, I needed a family and the young people of ECC took care of me. Likewise, sometimes things get tough for foreigners in Seoul and they need a family. The Christian family should not only be there for the tough times, but also to enjoy life together in a right way. The young people at ECC did many fun things together, and as simple as it sounds, I realized this was very important. In Seoul, the bars and clubs are always open. The world provides people with many opportunities to sin. I wondered how many opportunities the church was giving for young people to stand for God.

I created a group named "Called to Action." The main goal for this group was to constantly give young people an option to stand for Christ through creating a family of young believers. This family would be there to encourage and support each other. To give young people a reason not to go to the bars, we hosted movie nights, Karaoke nights, sports events, and more. I was more concerned for young people than I had ever been before. I met a lot of young people who were in Korea because they were running away from something at home. But they carried those burdens with them to Korea. The pressures of living in a foreign country, added to the struggles they already carried, left many struggling with depression.

During this time, I was introduced to a young lady. After talking for some time, we decided to go out for dinner. This dinner was supposed to be more like a date, but as we ate, my spirit was very troubled about this girl. I was trying so hard not to turn into a preacher on our first night out, so I did not say anything. We finished dinner and hung out by my university, and still my spirit was troubled. Then I start thinking, since my heart was focused on ministering to young people like her, maybe this was not a date but a ministry opportunity. I put my little feelings to the side, and I told her what was really on my heart. I told her what I thought she was going through and she perhaps was trying to medicate her struggles by seeing a boy. I told her that I didn't mean to put her on the spot, but I wanted to help her. I had troubles of my own and the Lord delivered me. He could do the same for her.

For a moment she was speechless. Then she looked me in the face, told me I was right and started to cry. A few moments later she told me the whole story. And then I gave her a testimony of what God can do to change our sorrows into joy. I am not going to be specific about what she was going through, but I will tell you that she went home that day with a heavy burden lifted from her shoulders. I promised to pray for her. A couple days later she called to tell me she was applying for a job, and I told her I would pray for that too. The next day she called and told me that she got the job. I told her God gave her the job, and all she needed to do was to let Him take care of her. A couple days later she called again and told me that she was going to church; as a matter of fact she later got into the church choir and started ministering through music. About two weeks later, she called again to thank me. She told me that the first night we met, she was so depressed with all the pressure and she was seriously contemplating suicide. That changed after we talked that day. God saved her life.

I met more young people that God used me to minister to in different ways. It is true many young people are hurting. According to different research studies, the most depressed age group of people is those between the ages of 19-35. Social life, family, work, and education all put so much pressure on young people and many, when they feel like they cannot handle the pressure, give up on life. It is surprising to find out that most suicide attempts are made by young people, who have a whole lifetime a head of them, instead of the old people whose lives are winding down.

It is also true that it is mostly young people who are running away from church, for very many different reasons. With all the depression and pressure young people endure, some run to church to encounter God, love, care and acceptance from the body of Christ. But there is a famine in some churches, because of this famine some people tend to do what Elimelech and Naomi did in *Ruth 1.*

"In the days when the judges ruled there was a famine in the land, and a man of Bethlehem in Judah went to sojourn in the country of Moab, he and his wife and his two sons. The name of the man was Elimelech and the name of his wife Naomi, and the names of his two sons were Mahlon and Chilion. They were Ephrathites from Bethlehem in Judah. They went into the country of Moab and remained there. But Elimelech, the husband of Naomi, died, and she was left with her two sons. These took Moabite wives; the name of the one was Orpah and the name of the other Ruth. They lived there about ten years, and both Mahlon and Chilion died, so that the woman was left without her two sons and her husband.

"Bethlehem" is made up of two words; "beth" means "house" and "lehem" means "bread." Bethlehem was the "house of bread," which was later the birth place of the Bread of Life. I look this bread not merely as food but as the bread of life, (Christ), or The Bread (the Word) in application to the church today. When there was no bread in the Bethlehem in the house of bread, it seemed a good reason for Elimelech and his family to leave. In the same way the when bread is lacking from our churches, many people might move on, the problem is that many migrate into the world (Moab). However it is in Moab that many young people are being killed every day, abortion, and all sorts of evil. It seems like a good idea to leave church but in the end it is like jumping from a frying pan into fire.

But God still loves us even when we run from Him, and He will still receive us when we turn away from our sins and run back to Him. *"Then she arose with her daughters-in-law to return from the country of Moab, for she had heard in the fields of Moab that the LORD had visited his people and given them food. So she set out from the place where she was with her two daughters-in-law, and they went on the way to return to the land of Judah (Ruth 1:1-7)."*

We need to run back to God because there is nothing in the world that can satisfy our hunger, but God. Naomi said in verse 21, "I left full but I came back empty" Being full does not mean having stuff, but having God is having it all. Naomi notes that despite the famine in Bethlehem-Judah, she was full but with all the bread in Moab she was empty. Away from God we are going to be empty, regardless of the stuff we have. I said all this to say that the major thing causing depression and death among young people is because many are empty because they ran away from God.

Running to God is a major step we can all take. After we embrace God, though, we have to embrace who He made us to be. From talking to a lot of young people, I have learned that, after running away from God, another great problem is people running away from themselves. They are running from who God made them to be. When you read beauty magazines or watch TV, you can see that there certain types of people are considered beautiful and others are considered ugly. There is a good body height and one that is bad. Maybe we do not have those body features that are considered beautiful. Maybe our eyes, nose, height, hair or weight are different. Then we hear society tell us we are not beautiful or acceptable, because we are not like the people on TV. This has pushed many young people to hate themselves, try to change themselves and desire to be something else. But trying to become someone else will never bring true happiness. I believe that joy begins with us embracing God and embracing who He made us to be. I have often shared the story below, from *Judges 3*, to help young people in this light.

"And the people of Israel again did what was evil in the sight of the LORD, and the LORD strengthened Eglon the king of Moab against Israel, because they had done what was evil in the sight of the LORD. He gathered to himself the Ammonites and the Amalekites, and went and defeated Israel. And they took possession of the city of palms. And the people of Israel served Eglon the king of Moab eighteen years.

"Then the people of Israel cried out to the LORD, and the LORD raised up for them a deliverer, Ehud, the son of Gera, the Benjaminite, a left-handed man. The people of Israel sent tribute by him to Eglon the king of Moab" (Judges 3:12-15).

Being left-handed was not a good thing back in the Bible times. It was considered a curse, and left-handed people were thought to be somewhat strange. But when the Bible says he was left-handed, it could also mean that his right hand was crippled, and he had no choice but use his left.

Despite what others saw as a flaw, Ehud was not a mistake. God had a purpose in making Ehud left-handed. When God was looking to deliver the children of Israel from the evil King Eglon, He chose this strange man Ehud to do the job. Ehud's purpose was hidden in his uniqueness; he was a left-handed man! Basically he needed to walk into the palace and kill King Eglon in order to free the children of Israel. He was going to use a dagger to kill King Eglon; I guess they did not have snipers back then. When packing a knife for battle, a right-handed man would put his dagger on his left thigh and vice versa. And since most people were right-handed, the king's security only checked guest's left side when making sure they were not carrying anything that could harm the king. The same applied to Ehud. When he was searched, security thought he was carrying nothing.

Many people will fail to see the anointing and the gifts we are blessed with because they are busy looking at what seems wrong in our lives. It could be that they see nothing in us, like they saw nothing on Ehud. In reality, as with Ehud, they are not looking in the right place. God blesses us in many ways that human eyes cannot see.

Ehud walked in with his dagger hidden on his right thigh, pulled it out and killed evil King Eglon. Because of the thing that made him different, he was able to deliver the children of Israel. God created us differently, and He gave us each unique gifts that He wants us to share with the world. We should not run away from who we are. In order to reach God's purpose in our lives, we must embrace the way He has made us.

Once school started, in March 2010, I spent less time reaching out to young people. As a fulltime freshman, I needed to spend a lot of time studying. As a new student, sometimes things got hard. One person was always there for me and I owe all my gratitude to him. He is the chaplain of Myongji University and the reason I came to this school. I visited his office on many different occasions. He once invited me into his home to celebrate Chuseok (Korean Thanksgiving) with his family. His wife made the best rice cakes. This man has been my mentor, my friend, my pastor and father. Chaplain Koo has been my hero at Myongji University. This gentlemen has a big heart.

I love Chaplain Koo, and for a very long time, I have prayed for him every day. He will forever have a special place in my heart. Chaplain Koo believes in me. Once there was a very special event at Onnuri Church, a huge church in Seoul. The president of Myongji was one of the honored guests there. Hundreds were in attendance, and the event was broadcast to thousands more. For this event, Chaplain Koo chose me to speak. It takes a lot of trust, in that situation, to give the microphone to a young man like me. He believed that I could do it, even when I did not. I was nervous as I got up to speak, but Chaplain Koo was sitting at the front row cheering for me to be bold and proclaim the Word of God. Any credit, for me being able to speak before all those people, should go to him.

That was not the only time Chaplain Koo gave me an opportunity to speak before people. We have a ceremony at Myongji, where the professors imitate Jesus in serving others. The professors washed the students' feet during this ceremony. Chaplain Koo chose me to speak at that ceremony. He told me that I had done a great job at Onnuri Church, and he said he believed I could do even better this time. I stood up to speak before the students, and this time I was more confident. Chaplain Koo sat at the front row again and prayed for me as I delivered the message.

I can't say enough about this gentleman. There are many times when I was quite discouraged with all the pressure I was feeling. I would walk into Chaplain Koo's office, and he would offer me some cool grape juice and talk to me. No matter how sad and hopeless I felt walking in, I always left his office with a smile. Chaplain Koo is a great pastor, teacher and missionary, and if it was not for the age difference I would say he is an awesome friend to me. I always pray for God's blessings him and his family.

While attending Myongji, I have had some other awesome experiences outside school. Someone contacted me and explained that he had heard that I could speak Korean well. He wondered whether he could introduce me to an agent at KBS TV. He said that there might be an opportunity for me to be in a TV drama. I said yes even before he finished speaking. This would be awesome for many reasons: I would get paid, I would be on TV, and I would make my language teacher proud. It worked out well. I auditioned and was cast as an extra in a couple of TV dramas. The first one was called Smile (웃어라 동해야). The other two were Rooftop Prince (왕세자) and Beautiful My Lady (아름다운 그녀). These were three incredible opportunities to meet some stars and be on TV. I was a little famous at school for a while.

The best part about joining Myongji was that I began a new journey of love with the most beautiful girl I ever met. It all started with a simple smile, her kindness and my desire to learn more Korean language. She kindly spent time helping me study Korean and I helped her with English. The first gift she ever gave me was a note book so I could write all my new Korean words; I still have that note book. I worked hard to improve my Korean, but this young lady was a major reason for my vast improvements with the language. We spent a lot of time studying, talking, playing and sometimes going to church together. There was nothing better in the world than spending time with her. I always dreamt that love would come and find me. A lady would walk into my life and blow me away. I never knew when she would come or what she would look like. I was captivated by this young woman, and I started thinking that she was the girl in my dreams.

Things got even better when I told her about how I felt. She said she felt the same way, though maybe not as crazy as me. We spent even more time together. My phone bills skyrocketed from all the texts I sent her. We were very happy to be around each other. I would have a rough day at school, but everything would be okay once I saw her. Talking to this girl was one thing that made my days brighter; it was the best thing about my days. She became everything to me. I thought she was the special one God had prepared for me. I had very little money, but I did not mind spending it on her just to make her happy. I preferred skipping lunch tomorrow in order to buy her a nice meal and seeing her happy today. She is the one person in the world for whom I would do anything. The Nesters and S were special to me, but this girl surpassed them all.

This was my first time officially in a relationship. I was so fearful, though. In the past it seemed like I had been separated from everyone I loved. The influenced my thinking in this relationship. I was extremely jealous when she talked to other boys. As crazy as it might sound, sometimes I was even jealous that she enjoyed time with her girlfriends. We would get into fights over nothing and they were entirely my fault. I was so jealous and insecure, always looking for proof that she would never leave me. Some of my most beautiful memories are of times spent with her. I did things for her that I have never done for anyone else. I loved her more than I ever loved anyone. There are no words to explain how much she meant to me. However, it did not last. Even though God had different plans than I had, I still pray for her and I am thankful for the time we shared together.

Over time, I made more excellent friendships at YongNak Church. One person God used in my life was an older friend, Sean Fitzwilliam. I have always desired a father figure in my life, someone older who would talk to me like a father would talk to a son. Sean spent a lot of time talking to me. On many occasions, I cried on his shoulder. Especially when I was struggling in my spiritual walk, I would go to his house and he would pray with me. He had such a father's heart, and he was a special gift for me from God. Sean let me stay at his house for some time. He taught me how to make lasagna, though I don't think I remember anymore. This man was so enthusiastic about his faith. Sadly, he is no longer in Korea, but Sean played a vital role in my life as a father figure, mentor and a great friend.

A very special couple in my life was Cory and Jen Dyck. Cory was not as old as Sean, but he became my mentor after Sean left. He became my best friend, and I spent more time with him than anyone else in the church. I also joined the Bible study he was attending. Cory was the only person I trusted with my deepest secrets. We often prayed together, I confessed my sins to Cory and he helped me work through them. Cory was always there for me when I needed to talk. I felt like I was a part of his family. When I stayed in the dorms at school every, now and then, I would get so sick of my roommates. Cory always let me sleep over, and Jen made the best breakfasts in the morning. Cory taught me how to play Xbox, especially the FIFA game that I now love.

During this time, I made another significant move. After much prayer and counsel, Pastor Bill and I agreed that I would move from YongNak Presbyterian Church to Seoul International Baptist Church (SIBC) under the leadership of Pastor Dan Armistead. Around the same time, Cory and Jen decided to change churches, too. One of the churches they visited was SIBC. They soon became members, so we still were able to worship together every Sunday. On one of the Sundays, I was given the chance to share my entire testimony during the service. It was very scary, but seeing Cory and Jen in the congregation encouraged me to speak boldly.

Cory and Jen had a dog named Sneakers. In Africa I always enjoyed having animals around me. Thanks to my friends, I could play with an animal again. Sneakers was always so much fun. Cory would also stay up late with me watching the English Premiere League. We both supported Arsenal. Even though he was very tired sometimes, he would still watch games with me. Cory and Jen had a little baby girl. Esther is the cutest little girl. Cory told her I was Uncle Mo. It felt so good; I actually felt like an uncle and a part of Cory's family. Even when his parents visited Korea, I spent a good deal of time with them, too. Cory and Jen truly were family to me.

Unfortunately, as with so many foreigners in Korea, Cory and Jen had to move back to America. During Bible study, it was so hard to imagine that I was not going to see Cory again for a very long time. Maybe never again. Korea would not be the same without my friend. I cried as I helped them pack for America. Early the morning before their flight, I went to McDonald's for one last meal with Cory and to say goodbye. To this day, though, our friendship is intact. Cory will forever have a special place in my heart. They are expecting a baby boy, and I promised Cory that I would teach his son to play basketball. So I hope that, sometime in the future, I will be able to meet Dyck Junior.

One of the first opportunities I was given to speak on the US army base was at a youth gathering called "Club Beyond." Randy Merkes led this group. This night was a blessing because God worked, and a couple of students came forward to accept Christ as their Lord and Savior. But this night was also very difficult for me; some of the kids there were the most undisciplined kids I have ever met. As I was sharing I mentioned that I had ten sisters back in Uganda. One of the kids made a very obscene comment about my sisters. As a man, in my culture, it is my duty to protect my sisters. I do not wish for any many to disrespect my sisters like that. I heard this comment while I was sharing about God's love, but I felt like I wanted to hurt this boy.

It was so hard time to keep my cool and let the Spirit work in my life after hearing a comment like that, but God enabled me to speak in love and forgiveness. In the end, that young boy was one of the few that walked up to receive Christ. The enemy is always working to disrupt us as we serve God. The enemy probably wanted to derail me with that comment. Whenever the enemy attacks us, we should always put God before our feelings and problems. God is to be lifted high and not ourselves.

One of the volunteers that event was a man named Daniel Lathrop. As I waiting for Randy Merkes to sign me off post, Daniel walked out and said, "Emmanuel, if you need any help you can always come to me." He gave me his phone number, but I had learnt a long time ago that people say that just to be nice. They do not actually mean that you should call them and say, "I did not eat today; please give me money for food." I took his number, but I had no intention of calling Daniel for anything, and for a very long time I did not.

SIBC gave me some awesome ministry opportunities, and the one that touched my heart the most was ministering to North Korean students. These students somehow escaped the home country and made their way to

South Korea. Their school was one of the ministries that SIBC supported. I went out to Sindo Island, while the students were camping there. Some American missionaries were also there. Looking at these students, I saw myself. I understood their actions. They would not really listen to the Americans; they would kind of isolate themselves, and they were very rough in their actions. I told these kids that I was not different from them. I had gone through rejection the same as they had. Maybe their government had failed them, but I told them that it was my own father that had rejected me. They connected somehow with me. They sat and listened and understood what I said. I was able to share God's love with them.

SIBC provided me for pocket money to support me as a student, and they provided me with my first house in Seoul. For their support I am grateful. But as I write this, I December I will finish my final exams, and I will wait to graduate in February. I will close the chapter of my life as a graduate student. The next chapter, which I consider the most important to me, is to join seminary and study God's word. I will be looking and praying for a seminary that will offer me a full ride scholarship or a church that will support me through seminary. Seminary will help me learn deeper about God's word, and I hope it will prepare me to step out and teach the Word.

CHAPTER 26

A FINAL LESSON

As I write this, I am out on a mission trip in a small Korean city called Taebaek. I gave a devotional this morning, and I want to share it with you. It is about the spirit of gratitude. Through the journey that I have been on, and the love that I have received, my final lesson is gratitude.

"On the way to Jerusalem he was passing along between Samaria and Galilee. And as he entered a village, he was met by ten lepers, who stood at a distance and lifted up their voices, saying, 'Jesus, Master, have mercy on us.' When he saw them he said to them, 'Go and show yourselves to the priests.' And as they went they were cleansed. Then one of them, when he saw that he was healed, turned back, praising God with a loud voice; and he fell on his face at Jesus' feet, giving him thanks. Now he was a Samaritan. Then Jesus answered, 'Were not ten cleansed? Where are the nine? Was no one found to return and give praise to God except this foreigner?' And he said to him, 'Rise and go your way; your faith has made you well'" (Luke 17:11-19).

Of the nine who were healed, only one comes back to thank Jesus for healing him. And he wasn't even a Jew. This grateful man was a Samaritan. I might be wrong, but this is the only place in the Bible where I see someone come back to Jesus simply to thank him. We see all kinds of people around Jesus, but most of them want something from him. They need healing or someone they know has a need. But this time, even though this man first encountered Jesus as a needy person, now he has come back as a grateful man. Many of us Christians today suffer from a spirit of entitlement, thinking God should give us this and that. Some churches preach that God must bless you, prosper you, heal your sicknesses and do other things you want. We lack the spirit of gratitude. We think we deserve good health and all the blessings. If God gave us what we all truly deserve, though, none of us would like it.

Sometimes we expect things from God. Sometimes we take Him for granted. We grow accustomed to His blessings. When you get food every day, we easily forget to be thankful for it. Those who don't often have food have a great spirit of gratitude when they receive a good meal.

In Luke, there were ten lepers. They all had the same problem, and they all prayed. Nine, however, missed the opportunity to praise. Only one saw the reason to praise. Only one truly understood what Jesus had done for him. Many of us sense a great need to pray and cry out to God, but we rarely feel the need to praise God. All ten lepers had a reason to praise God, but only one recognized it and acted upon it. The same is true in our lives. We have reason to praise God, but often we would rather whine instead of being grateful.

We might be going through some problems, but if we look back, we can see that God has done so much for us. We ought to forever be thankful. As I write this, I have been meditating on how far God has brought me. He has done so much for me, and I should forever praise the Lord.

What is more amazing about this Samaritan man is the way he approached Jesus this second time. When he first caught Jesus' attention, it was in a loud voice. He used that same voice, the very same fervor, when he came back to express his gratitude. This changed my practice a lot, because I am guilty of the opposite. I have often gone crazy praying for God me provide for me, heal me or take care of me, but seldom have I gone crazy giving God praise for hearing and answering my prayers. We fast and go to great lengths when asking God to give us a job or baby or a cure for our illness, but when those things come, perhaps we put some cash in the offering basket and think that should show our thankfulness.

This man understood that he was rejected by his family and friends, was branded unclean, lived a life of solace, and no one could come to help him. No physician or doctor would help him except Jesus. Jesus was the only one who cared enough to hear and respond when these men cried out for help.

This man understood that he would never get anywhere close to his family. Death was in his face as leprosy, slowly but surely, ate his body. He knew well the feelings of rejection and uncleanness. When he saw the goodness of Jesus, he was compelled to turn around to go give praise. Many of us focus too much time on the blessing and forget the One who blesses. Many of us of have praised our cars, our children, our homes and our churches, but have neglected to praise God who has provided all these things.

Like the healed leper, I want to give glory now to God for what He has done for me. When I was in a bad place, isolated from God and destined for eternal separation from Him, Christ came and took all my sins upon Himself. He did it so that I could have a relationship with the Father in heaven, and for this I will be forever grateful to my Lord Jesus Christ. When I became a believer in Christ and my family and friends left me, Christ was right there with me. He provided for me and wiped away my tears. When everyone else counted me out and called me names, God said, "You are the apple of my eye. I love you, and you are my beloved son." Many times I have messed up, even as a Christian. Even church people judged me and kicked me out of their fellowship, but Christ was always there. Even when I ran away from Him, He was there. When I acted like I did not know Him, Jesus was always there loving me and caring for me. For this I am very thankful. God brought me from Uganda and got my visa for Korea. He provided food for, shelter and a school for me in Korea. He has given me peace that surpasses all human understanding. In situations where I should be falling apart, Christ gives me the peace that keeps me stable. He gave me favor before friends and many others in Myonji University, YongNak Church and Seoul International Baptist Church. It was all Jesus Christ and I want to give the glory and honor to Him. I want to say thank you. I pray that God will give me the grace to live a life of gratitude for the rest of my days.

Printed in the United States
By Bookmasters